READ and Reflect

2

Academic Reading Strategies and Cultural Awareness

Lori Howard

with Jayme Adelson-Goldstein

OXFORD
UNIVERSITY PRESS

OXFORD
UNIVERSITY PRESS

198 Madison Avenue
New York, NY 10016 USA

Great Clarendon Street
Oxford OX2 6DP England

Auckland   Bangkok   Buenos Aires   Cape Town   Chennai
Dar es Salaam   Delhi   Hong Kong   Istanbul   Karachi   Kolkata
Kuala Lumpur   Madrid   Melbourne   Mexico City   Mumbai
Nairobi   São Paulo   Shanghai   Taipei   Tokyo   Toronto

OXFORD is a trademark of Oxford University Press

ISBN 0-19-437730-X

Copyright © 2004 Oxford University Press

Library of Congress Cataloging-in-Publication Data

Howard, Lori (Lori B.)
    Read and reflect 2: academic reading strategies and cultural awareness /
Lori Howard with Jayme Adelson-Goldstein.
        p. cm.
    ISBN 0-19-437730-X
    1. English language—Textbooks for foreign speakers. 2. College readers.
I. Title: Read and reflect two. II. Adelson-Goldstein, Jayme. III. Title.

PE1128.H6275 2005
428.6'4—dc22   2004054772

Editorial Manager: Janet Aitchison
Senior Editor: Pietro Alongi
Associate Editor: Ashli Totty
Art Director: Lynn Luchetti
Design Project Manager: Maj-Britt Hagsted
Senior Designer: Claudia Carlson
Designer: Michael Steinhofer
Layout Artist: Julie Macus
Art Editor: Judi DeSouter
Production Manager: Shanta Persaud
Production Controller: Eve Wong

Printing (last digit): 10 9 8 7 6 5 4 3 2 1

Printed in Hong Kong

Acknowledgements

Illustrations: Barbara Bastian pp 9–10, 29–30, 73–74, 77–78; Linda Fong
pp. 1, 77; Paul Hampson pp. 49, 65, 81, 88.

*The publishers would like to thank the following for their permission to
reproduce photographs and cartoons:* ©1989 Edward Koren from
Cartoonbank.com p. 33.; ©1994 Mort Gerberg from Cartoonbank.com
p. 59.; ©1973 Al Ross from Cartoonbank.com p. 75.; ©1999 Robert
Mankoff from Cartoonbank.com p. 113.; CORBIS p. 8. Jacob A. Riis, p. 25.;
Courtesy of State Museum Resource Center, California State Parks p. 8.; Joe
Putrock p. 13.; Printed by permission of the Norman Rockwell Family

Agency copyright ©1961 The Norman Rockwell Family Entities p. 17.;
Barbara Munson p. 28.; Alamy: Alexandra Carlile/Elvele Images p. 30.;
Jodi Waxman/OUP p. 43.; AgeFoto Stock: Rich Pomerantz p. 43.; Digital
Vision pp. 100–101.; Antonio Sacre p. 73.; Getty Images: Andy Sacks p.
89.; U.S. Forest Service and the National Association of State Foresters
p. 94.; U.S. Department of Transportation's National Highway Traffic
Safety Administration p. 94.; Cartoonstock.com: Nick Baker
p. 97.; Dennis McGlynn p.104.; Index Stock: Elektra Vision/Image
Source p. 108.; No Limits and Eric Perlman p. 109.

Special thanks: John Mole, Karen Minot (realia backgrounds).

*The publishers would also like to thank the following for their permission
to adapt and reproduce copyright material:* **pp. 9–10.** "A Larger
Memory: A History of Our Diversity with Voices" used by permission
of Janet Gilmore; **pp. 12–13.** "Moving Up in the World, Northward,"
by Tania Padgett, copyright © 2003 Newsday, represented by Tribune
Media Services International; **p. 25.** From THE COLLECTED POEMS
OF LANGSTON HUGHES by Langston Hughes, copyright © 1994 by
The Estate of Langston Hughes. Used by permission of Alfred A. Knopf,
a division of Random House, Inc. Reprinted by permission of Harold
Ober Associates Incorporated. Copyright © 1994 by The Estate of
Langston Hughes; **pp. 29–30.** © NPR ® 2002. Any unauthorized
duplication is strictly prohibited; **pp. 52–53.** This article appeared in the
August 1996 issue and is reprinted with permission from *The World & I*,
a publication of The Washington Times Corporation, copyright © 1996;
pp. 60–61. This article appeared in the March 1999 issue and is reprinted
with permission from *The World & I*, a publication of The Washington
Times Corporation, copyright © 1999; **pp. 68–69.** "Soulful Eating is an
Aid to the Body and Spirit" by Gurney Williams III, used by permission
of the Minneapolis Star Tribune; **pp. 73–74.** "My Last Meal" used by
permission of Antonio Sacre; **pp. 77–78** used by permission of Slow
Food USA; **pp. 84–85.** © 2002 *World Book Encyclopedia*; **pp. 104–105.**
Reprinted courtesy of SPORTS ILLUSTRATED: "Lovers Leap" by Lars
Anderson, October 15, 2001. Copyright © 2001, Time Inc. All rights
reserved; "Think Success and Hang In There", by Gary Hook, copyright
© 2001, USA TODAY; **pp. 120–121.** Copyright © 2002 by The New
York Times Co. Reprinted with permission.

*The Publisher would like to acknowledge the following individuals
for their invaluable input during the development of this series:*
Jane Selden, Steven Brown, Deborah Lazarus, Leann Howard, Robert
Irwin, Nick Lambert, Jean Rose, Yara Maria Bannwart Rago, Julie Un,
Anthea Tillyer, Lynne Barsky, Daryl Kinney, Elizabeth Neblett, Carol
Curtis, Gail August, Betsy Gilliland, Anita Gaye Childress, Laura Walsh,
David Ross, Kathy Sherak, Christine Tierney, Glória K. Delbim, Rob
Waring

Author Acknowledgements

The authors gratefully acknowledge the skill and dedication of the Oxford
staff who worked on Read and Reflect—Janet Aitchison, Stephanie
Karras, Pietro Alongi, Amy Cooper, Daria Ruzicka and Ashli Totty—and
of the design team. Their hard work shows on every page.

Much gratitude goes to Gary and Emily Goldstein, Lindsay, Eric and
Greg Wolff, Michael Howard, Julie Barnard, Deena Altman, Barry Bakin,
Giang Hoang, Antonio Sacre, Kathryn Baron, Reporter—KQED Public
Radio News, San Francisco, and the reference librarians of the Mill
Valley and Corte Madera Libraries.

Dedication

This book is dedicated to Jayme Adelson-Goldstein: brilliant teacher,
creative author, splendid writing partner and treasured friend.—LH

Introduction

Welcome to *Read and Reflect: Academic Reading Strategies and Cultural Awareness*

This reading series for high-beginning and intermediate students of English as a second or foreign language has four key goals:

- to develop students' awareness and use of reading strategies
- to increase their academic vocabulary, thus preparing them to read academic texts
- to provide a forum for students to learn about and discuss aspects of American culture
- to increase students' enjoyment of the reading process through a wealth of high-interest texts

This book is ideal for young adults planning to pursue a college education; however, it can also be used by students who want to improve their reading skills to attain a personal goal or to advance in the workplace.

Read and Reflect teaches students to read with purpose and comprehension and to interact with the text as they read. In each unit of *Read and Reflect*, students are introduced to a new strategy that supports the target reading skill (for example, looking at the title and source of a text is a strategy for previewing). Exercises throughout the book have students apply these strategies as they read. Activities in both levels help students develop reading fluency. Level 2 also has specific exercises to develop reading speed.

How This Book is Organized

Read and Reflect contains eight thematic units, each tied to a cultural concept such as diversity, consumer awareness, and sports. To maximize reading opportunities, each unit contains four texts adapted from authentic sources. These texts have different topics, but are connected to the overall cultural theme. Cartoons, questionnaires, charts, and narrative paragraphs provide additional reading practice.

At the beginning of each unit, the cultural theme and reading goals are introduced. Students are asked what they know about the theme and then discuss their prior knowledge, thoughts, and ideas. Pre-reading activities throughout the book provide background information, key vocabulary, and critical reading strategies that enhance students' comprehension of the texts.

All texts are followed by processing activities that require students to demonstrate their understanding, and to use their higher-level thinking skills to analyze and synthesize new information. Because active vocabulary development is an important part of developing reading proficiency, vocabulary exercises occur throughout the units.

A key feature of each unit is the Read and Share activity. Students read one of two related texts in order to share and discuss what they learned. This activity gives students an enhanced purpose for reading while also providing them with an opportunity to apply the reading strategies they have learned.

At the end of each unit, students reflect on what they have read through three expansion activities: an interview, a charting activity, and a writing activity.

Special Features of this Series

- Academic reading strategies
- Academic vocabulary
- Reading skills and vocabulary recycled from unit to unit
- Adapted authentic materials
- Strategies to improve reading speed
- Collaborative learning opportunities
- Critical literacy development

A more detailed description of these features and the unit activities is included in the Teacher's Notes on page 135. The Answer Key begins on page 129.

We hope you find *Read and Reflect* a useful and enjoyable teaching tool. We welcome your comments and ideas. Please write to us care of:
Oxford University Press
English Language Teaching Division
198 Madison Avenue
New York, New York 10016

Lori Howard and Jayme Adelson-Goldstein

Contents

Cultural Concept	Reading Skill	Vocabulary Objective
Immigration	**Previewing and Predicting:** Preview key elements (title, headings, etc.) to determine what you already know about a text. Then predict what you will learn.	Use the suffix *-ion*.
Diversity	**Previewing:** Preview comprehension questions to help you predict what you will read about and pay attention to important ideas and details as you read.	Distinguish between verbs, nouns, and adjectives in word families.
Appearance	**Scanning:** Use signals such as capital letters, numbers or symbols (%, @, etc.) to help you scan for information.	Distinguish between adjectives and adverbs in word families.
Media	**Using Context Clues:** Use clues (e.g., synonyms, definitions, examples, or contrasts) to help you understand unknown vocabulary.	Distinguish between nouns and adjectives in word families. Use context clues to understand unknown vocabulary.
Food	**Identifying the Main Idea and Supporting Details:** Find the main ideas in a text and discriminate between main ideas and supporting details.	Use context clues to understand unknown vocabulary. Distinguish between nouns and adjectives in word families.
Consumer Awareness	**Summarizing:** Use the main idea and supporting details to help you write a short version of a text.	Use the prefix *un-*. Use context clues to understand unknown vocabulary.
Sports	**Skimming:** Move your eyes quickly down a page, not reading every word, in order to get an idea of what the text is about.	Distinguish between action, person, and topic in word families.
Communication	**Identifying Patterns of Organization:** Recognize patterns such as lists and sequences to help you understand and remember what you read.	Use context clues to understand unknown vocabulary.

To the Student

Dear Student,

Welcome to *Read and Reflect*. The purpose of this series is to help you improve your reading in English. You will:

- learn **reading strategies** that will prepare you to read academic or college texts.
- increase your **vocabulary** so that you will better understand what you read.
- discuss **cultural issues** presented in the texts.

Read and Reflect has thirty-two texts on topics such as diversity, consumer awareness, and extreme sports. These texts come from newspapers, magazines, textbooks, websites, biographies, and encyclopedias. To help you improve your reading, each unit of the book asks you to follow three basic steps: **Get Ready to Read, Read,** and **Process What You Read**.

A Word about Reading Strategies

You use reading strategies to help you understand and remember what you read. Some strategies such as previewing and predicting prepare you to read a text. Other strategies, such as scanning and skimming, help you get information from the text without reading every word. Each time you learn a strategy in this book, practice it as often as you can.

Some Suggestions to Help you Read Better

- Decide what you want to find out from the text before you read it.
- Think about what you already know about the topic.
- Look at the title, picture, and headings to help you guess what you will learn from the text.
- Read silently and try not to say the words in your mind or move your lips
- While you read ask yourself questions such as *Is this true? Do I agree with this? What does this mean to me?*
- Skip over vocabulary words you don't know. (You will be surprised at how much you understand.)
- After you read, check your understanding. Use the questions after the text or your own questions such as *What do I know now? What is my opinion of the author's ideas?*

A Word about Reading Speed

Reading faster will improve your comprehension. You will be surprised at how much you understand even when you read quickly. Try to read faster each time you read. It also helps to read as often as you can. The more you read, the better and faster you'll read!

We wish you a life filled with good books, good health, and good times.

Lori Howard and Jayme Adelson-Goldstein

Unit 1

The American Quilt

In this unit you will:

- read about immigration in the U.S.
- learn how to preview and make predictions about a text
- practice identifying common words

WHAT DO YOU KNOW ABOUT IMMIGRATION?

A. Look at the picture. What is the artist's message? Discuss your ideas with your classmates.

B. Think about these questions. Discuss your answers with a partner. Then share your ideas with your classmates.

1. Why do people immigrate to a new country? Give five reasons.

2. What are the advantages and disadvantages of living in a country with many immigrants?

1 GET READY TO READ ABOUT: Immigration

A. Answer the questions below. Then survey nine classmates. Use tick marks (⊮⊮) to record all the responses.

THE IMMIGRANT EXPERIENCE			
Is it difficult to . . .	Yes	Somewhat	No
1. live far from family and friends?			
2. learn a new way of life?			
3. change jobs or careers?			
4. learn a new language?			
5. eat new foods?			

B. Discuss the results of your survey with your classmates. Use the following expressions:

Nine out of ten people . . .
More than half of the people . . .
Only a few people . . .

C. Work with a partner. Read these sentences about an immigrant family. Guess which word or phrase has a meaning similar to the underlined word or phrase in each sentence. Check your guesses after you read the article on pages 4–5.

1. When Elena and Sam Rios immigrated to the United States, they brought their Guatemalan <u>customs</u> with them.

   (a.) traditions   b. books   c. carpets

2. They liked the <u>diversity</u> in U.S. schools. Their children's classmates were from all over the world.

   a. variety of students   b. number of students   c. amount of students

3. They wanted to <u>assimilate into</u> American society, so they went to American stores, ate American food, and watched American TV shows.

   a. be different from   b. be separate from   c. become a part of

4. Elena and Sam wanted to <u>contribute</u> something to their new country. They helped start a community center in their neighborhood.

   a. take   b. give   c. demonstrate

5. They also tried to <u>preserve</u> their culture by speaking Spanish *and* English at home and celebrating Guatemalan holidays.

   a. keep   b. throw out   c. change

2 BUILDING READING SKILLS: Previewing and Predicting

> Previewing and predicting are reading skills you can use *before* you read a text. When you **preview**, you look at key elements, such as the title or headings, that give you important information about what you will read. Then you use these same elements to **predict**, or guess, what you will learn in the text.

Practice Previewing and Predicting

Preview the key elements of the text. Work with a partner to answer the questions below.

Dr. Wolff discusses immigration trends and how they will affect the future of the U.S.

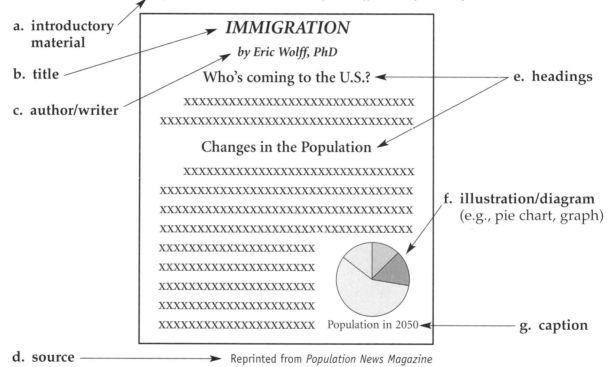

a. introductory material

b. title

c. author/writer

IMMIGRATION

by Eric Wolff, PhD

Who's coming to the U.S.?

Changes in the Population

e. headings

f. illustration/diagram (e.g., pie chart, graph)

Population in 2050

g. caption

d. source — Reprinted from *Population News Magazine*

1. What is the title of this text?

2. Based on the introductory material, what is the topic of the text? What do you already know about this topic?

3. Who is the author? What is the source?

4. What do you already know about the topic of each heading?

5. What information do the pie chart and caption give?

6. Based on your preview, what do you predict you will learn in this text?

Use Your Reading Skills

Take one minute to preview the key elements of the article below. Then complete these statements. Check your answers as you read the article.

1. From the title, I know this article is about . . .

2. From the introductory material and headings, I know the article discusses . . .

3. From the pie charts, I know the article has information about . . .

4. Based on my preview, I predict I will learn . . .

3 READ

This textbook article traces the history of immigration in the U.S. and discusses the effect immigration has on American culture.

IMMIGRANTS IN THE UNITED STATES—A POT, A QUILT, A CHOIR

The Melting Pot

In the 20th century, people called the United States a melting pot of cultures. This meant that they looked
5 at the country as a place where immigrants' customs and traditions came together to form one single American culture. In the early 1900s this seemed to be true. When new
10 immigrants arrived, many of them tried to assimilate quickly because they wanted to fit into the new culture. They believed that to be successful, they had to take on
15 American customs and leave their own customs behind. However, by the end of the 20th century, this way of thinking began to change. Today many immigrants are holding on to
20 their first languages and cultures as they learn English and the customs of their new home.

20th-Century Immigration

The term *melting pot* comes from
25 Israel Zangwill's 1908 play of the same name. When Zangwill wrote his play, the United States was experiencing the largest increase in immigration in its history. Between
30 1890 and 1920, 18 million people (mostly Europeans from Italy, Germany, Ireland, England, and Poland) came to the U.S. Immigrants studied English and worked hard to
35 take part in the American dream—the opportunity to have a good job, a good education, and a good future for their children. In addition, they contributed their skills, ideas, and hard work to
40 American society. They also added their traditions, customs, and foods to the "pot." The image[1] of the melting pot was the model for immigrants in the United States in the last century.

[1] **image:** a mental picture of something

New Century, New Immigrants

Now the United States is facing a new wave of immigrants, mostly from Asia and Latin America, rather than from Europe. Experts predict that by 2065 there will be almost 450 million people in the country, and one out of every three people will be either Hispanic[2] or Asian. "We are on our way to becoming the first country in history that is made up of every part of the world," says Kenneth Prewitt, former director of the U.S. Census Bureau.

In an "international" nation like the U.S., there is no longer a single cultural pot to melt into. Which culture should new immigrants choose? Many immigrant parents want their children to succeed in the United States, but they also want them to remember their first language and traditions. Unlike the immigrants in the early 20th century, these immigrants prefer to preserve their own culture rather than assimilate completely.

A New Image

It's clear from the new demographics[3] that it's time to replace the image of the melting pot with something else—perhaps a multicolored quilt,[4] or a choir with

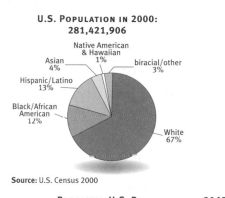

U.S. POPULATION IN 2000: 281,421,906

Native American & Hawaiian 1%
biracial/other 3%
Asian 4%
Hispanic/Latino 13%
Black/African American 12%
White 67%

Source: U.S. Census 2000

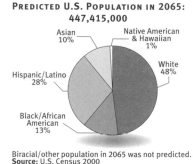

PREDICTED U.S. POPULATION IN 2065: 447,415,000

Asian 10%
Native American & Hawaiian 1%
White 48%
Hispanic/Latino 28%
Black/African American 13%

Biracial/other population in 2065 was not predicted.
Source: U.S. Census 2000

various voices singing together. Immigrants in this country have always had a great effect on their new home, influencing the music that Americans listen to, the food they eat, and the ideas they have. These contributions are an important part of the country's history and future. After all, it is the variety of cultures and ideas that gives the United States its energy and ability to grow and change. Whether pot, quilt, or choir, the United States of the 21st century is growing stronger, thanks to its great diversity.

[2] **Hispanic:** from a Spanish-speaking culture or country
[3] **demographics:** facts about the population of a specific area
[4] **quilt:** a cover for a bed, made of different pieces of colored cloth

A. **Read each statement and decide if it is true (T) or false (F). Look back at the article to check your answers.**

___T___ 1. Between 1890 and 1920, 18 million people immigrated to the United States.

_____ 2. In the early 20th century, new immigrants didn't want to learn U.S. customs.

_____ 3. The melting pot image showed that people believed in a single American culture.

_____ 4. Immigrants have contributed a lot to U.S. culture.

_____ 5. Today the majority of U.S. immigrants are from Europe.

_____ 6. In the 21st century, the U.S. is accepting fewer immigrants than in the past.

_____ 7. Today many immigrants prefer to keep their own culture and language.

_____ 8. Experts predict that in 2065, two out of every three people in the U.S. will be Asian.

B. **Using the pie charts in the article, write the correct percentages in the chart below. Then circle the ethnic group whose population will grow the most by 2065. Use the information to answer the questions below.**

U.S. POPULATION		
Ethnic group	**% in 2000**	**% in 2065**
Asian	4%	
Black/African American		
Hispanic/Latino		
Native American and Hawaiian		
White		

1. From 2000 to 2065, by how much will the numbers change for each group?
2. How do you think these changes will affect U.S. society?

C. **Think about these questions. Then discuss them with your classmates.**

1. What are some of the difficulties that immigrants face in the 21st century?
2. What are some ways a society can help immigrants preserve their first language and culture?

5 WORK WITH THE VOCABULARY

A. Match the words with their definitions. Look back at the article on pages 4–5 to check your answers.

_e_ **1.** assimilate   a. do something for, or give something to a society or group

____ **2.** preserve   b. the usual ways people do things

____ **3.** contribute   c. variety in race, culture, and religion

____ **4.** customs   d. keep or protect something

    5. diversity   e. become part of a group

Suffixes: *-ion*

You can use the suffix *-ion* to form nouns from some verbs. For example, *educate* means "to teach or give knowledge."

educate + -ion = education

Education is a noun that means "learning or the process of getting knowledge." (The *-e* at the end of the verb disappears.)

B. Choose the correct form of the word for each sentence.

1. a. The opportunity for a good (educate/(education)) is part of the American dream.

   b. Many immigrants also want to (educate/education) their children in the language and culture of their home country.

2. a. In the past, immigrants believed it was important to (assimilate/assimilation) into American society.

   b. The (assimilate/assimilation) process often takes many years.

3. a. (Immigrate/Immigration) continues to bring many people to the United States.

   b. The number of people who want to (immigrate/immigration) keeps growing.

4. a. Immigrants (contribute/contribution) to American society every day.

   b. Their (contribute/contributions) can be seen in every aspect of American life.

5. a. The (populate/population) of the United States will almost double in 65 years.

   b. Immigrants help (populate/population) various cities in the United States.

6 IMPROVING READING SPEED AND COMPREHENSION: Identifying Common Words

> **Common words** such as *in, on, it,* and *about* make up about 50 percent of the words in most texts. If you learn these words and are able to identify them quickly, you can increase your reading speed and comprehension. See the inside back cover for the list of the 100 Most Common Words.

Practice Identifying Common Words

In a small group, brainstorm 15 words you think are among the 100 most common English words. Then look at the list on the inside back cover and answer these questions.

1. How many of your words match the words on the list?

2. How many of the words on the list do you know?

3. Find words on the list you don't know. Have each member of your group look up these words in a dictionary and share the definitions.

7 GET READY TO READ ABOUT: Immigrants

A. **Look at the pictures. Where do you think these immigrants are from? When do you think they came to the United States? Why do you think they immigrated? Discuss your answers with your classmates.**

B. **Put a check (✓) next to the words you know. Ask your classmates for the meanings of the words you don't know. Look up the words no one knows in a dictionary.**

___ appreciate	___ diary	___ discrimination	___ failure
___ family album	___ honor	___ majority	___ role

Use Your Reading Skills

Take 30 seconds to preview the key elements of the article below. Then complete these statements. Compare answers with your classmates.

1. From the title, I know this type of article is called a . . .

2. From the introductory material, I know the article is about . . .

3. I predict I will learn . . .

8 READ

This book review discusses Ronald Takaki's A Larger Memory. *In his book, Takaki talks about how the diversity of the United States has contributed to the development of American culture.*

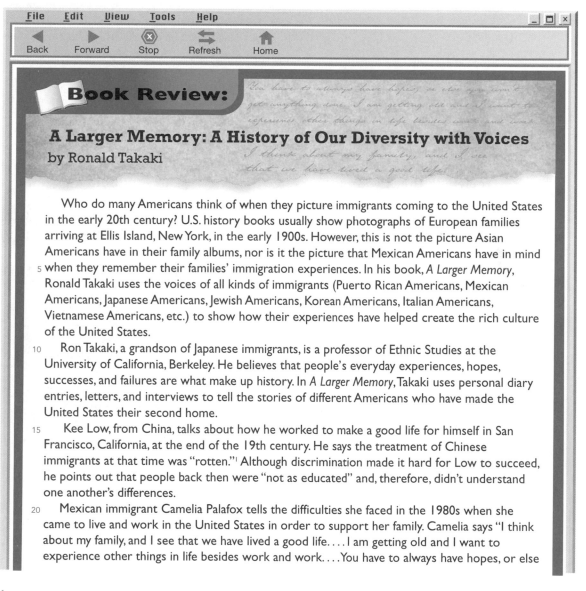

File   Edit   View   Tools   Help

◀ Back   ▶ Forward   ⊗ Stop   ⇄ Refresh   ⌂ Home

Book Review:

A Larger Memory: A History of Our Diversity with Voices
by Ronald Takaki

Who do many Americans think of when they picture immigrants coming to the United States in the early 20th century? U.S. history books usually show photographs of European families arriving at Ellis Island, New York, in the early 1900s. However, this is not the picture Asian Americans have in their family albums, nor is it the picture that Mexican Americans have in mind
5 when they remember their families' immigration experiences. In his book, *A Larger Memory*, Ronald Takaki uses the voices of all kinds of immigrants (Puerto Rican Americans, Mexican Americans, Japanese Americans, Jewish Americans, Korean Americans, Italian Americans, Vietnamese Americans, etc.) to show how their experiences have helped create the rich culture of the United States.

10 Ron Takaki, a grandson of Japanese immigrants, is a professor of Ethnic Studies at the University of California, Berkeley. He believes that people's everyday experiences, hopes, successes, and failures are what make up history. In *A Larger Memory*, Takaki uses personal diary entries, letters, and interviews to tell the stories of different Americans who have made the United States their second home.

15 Kee Low, from China, talks about how he worked to make a good life for himself in San Francisco, California, at the end of the 19th century. He says the treatment of Chinese immigrants at that time was "rotten."[1] Although discrimination made it hard for Low to succeed, he points out that people back then were "not as educated" and, therefore, didn't understand one another's differences.

20 Mexican immigrant Camelia Palafox tells the difficulties she faced in the 1980s when she came to live and work in the United States in order to support her family. Camelia says "I think about my family, and I see that we have lived a good life. . . . I am getting old and I want to experience other things in life besides work and work. . . . You have to always have hopes, or else

[1] **rotten:** very bad, unfair, unkind

you won't get anything done. That's how I see life." These ideas—hopes for a good life and the
25 hard work needed to achieve[2] it—echo again and again in the stories of different immigrants.

Professor Takaki hopes that his book will help Americans develop greater awareness[3] of other cultures and a sense of community. This is especially important now, he says, as the United States soon will be a country in which no single group forms a majority of the population. He believes that cultural diversity and the contributions of many immigrant groups are the main
30 reasons for America's prosperity[4] and success. Takaki wants people from all backgrounds to appreciate the roles they've had in making the United States what it is today. According to Takaki, when America learns to honor the contributions of each person and each group, everyone will feel that they're an important part of the country and its history.

Ronald Takaki is the author of several books including the Pulitzer Prize nominee A Different Mirror:
35 A History of Multicultural America. *Professor Takaki has lectured in many countries and has advised political leaders on racial matters.*

Adapted from the University of California, Berkeley website

[2] **achieve:** to be successful in doing or getting something
[3] **awareness:** knowledge or understanding
[4] **prosperity:** good fortune, wealth

9 PROCESS WHAT YOU READ

A. **Choose the best word or phrase to complete each sentence. Look back at the book review to check your answers.**

a. author	b. Europe	c. history	d. interviews
e. majority	f. Mexico and Asia	g. prosperity and success	h. succeed

1. History books usually show photos of immigrants from _b_ in the 1900s.

2. In the early 20th century, immigrants also came from ___ .

3. Ron Takaki is the ___ of *A Larger Memory*.

4. He uses diary entries, letters, and ___ to tell immigrants' stories.

5. He shows how immigrants work hard and ___ .

6. Takaki believes that people's ordinary experiences make up ___ .

7. Soon no single group in the United States will be a ___ .

8. In his book, Takaki says that cultural diversity is the main reason for America's ___ .

B. **Look at the third paragraph of the book review on page 9. Underline all the words you remember from the list of the 100 most common words. Then look at the list on the inside back cover to check your answers. The paragraph has 68 words. How many of them are common words?**

A. Work in small groups. Imagine you are moving to a new town. What do you hope to find there? What do you hope not to find there? Use the chart below to categorize the following situations. Then add your own ideas.

good schools	business opportunities	crime
discrimination	a diverse community	safe streets
affordable housing	crowded schools	high unemployment

What you hope to find	What you hope not to find
good schools	crowded schools

B. Put a check (✓) next to the words you know. Ask your classmates for the meanings of the words you don't know. Look up the words no one knows in a dictionary.

____ accomplish   ____ affordable   ____ convince   ____ entrepreneur

____ opportunity   ____ refugee   ____ rewarding   ____ thrive

C. Preview the key elements of the two texts on pages 12–14. Then answer these questions.

1. What is the topic of text A? What type of text is it?

2. What is the topic of text B? What type of text is it?

D. Choose one text to read. Then answer these questions.

1. What is the title of your text?

2. What do you already know about the topic?

3. What do you predict you will learn?

Each immigrant group helps shape American society. This newspaper article describes how one group, the Guyanese, is the hope of a city that has experienced hard times.

Schenectady,[1] New York

Ramesh Doodnauth never wanted to own a business and never dreamed of being an entrepreneur. For 16 years he
5 earned a good living, working in New York City's garment district.[2] However, when his two young daughters complained that they didn't see him enough, Doodnauth,
10 41, decided to stop working for someone else and become his own boss. He did it by moving to a small city three hours north of New York City — Schenectady.

15 In the early 1900s, hardworking Polish and Italian immigrants helped Schenectady grow and thrive. As the home of the General Electric Company, Schenectady was
20 known as the city that lights the world. By the end of the 20th century, however, Schenectady was a city without a future. Most of its manufacturing companies closed or
25 reduced their size, and many people lost their jobs. At that time, no one thought about moving to Schenectady; in fact, many people left the city to find work elsewhere.

30 Lately, however, things are looking better. Schenectady has become a place of opportunity for thousands of New York City's Guyanese Americans, who are
35 looking for affordable homes, better schools, and business opportunities. In 2002, about 2,500 Guyanese[3] immigrants, mostly from Queens, settled in Schenectady and
40 improved its local economy by buying homes and opening small businesses. "We started the ball rolling," laughs Savitrie Rajkumar, one of the first Guyanese to move.
45 She and her husband bought a run-down[4] house for $13,500 in 1998. They fixed it up and spread the word about Schenectady to friends and family back in Queens.

50 Doodnauth's experience in the garment industry didn't teach him much about running a business. However, he soon realized that a city with a growing Guyanese
55 population needed a store that sold Guyanese food. Doodnauth sold his home in Queens, bought a building in downtown Schenectady, and opened Timothy's World, a West
60 Indian grocery store that sells items such as parboiled rice, split peas, and Caribbean pinetart desserts.

Other Guyanese in Schenectady had the same idea. Kowsih and
65 Prakesh Mahabeer expanded their grocery store because demand for

---

[1] *Schenectady* is pronounced *Ska-**nek**-ta-dee*
[2] **garment district:** an area in a city where clothing is designed and manufactured
[3] There are 140,000 Guyanese in Queens, a part of New York City. They came from Guyana, a country in South America. Most Guyanese trace their roots back to India.
[4] **run-down:** in bad condition

West Indian products as well as Indian music and movies has grown. Recently, ten Guyanese businesses opened, and there are plans to open more.

Schenectady Mayor Albert P. Jurczynski is so pleased with how hardworking the city's newest citizens are that he gives bus tours for Guyanese people still living in Queens. On the tour the mayor points out the advantages of moving to Schenectady: the beautiful parks, the library and schools, and the homes for sale at good prices. He also promises to build a stadium for cricket—a favorite sport in Guyana— once Schenectady's Guyanese population reaches 50,000. Yasmin Baksh, took the bus tour and commented, "We feel so welcome. They want us to come develop the area."

Mayor Jurczynski is happy that the Guyanese are helping his city. "Schenectady was dying," said Jurczynski. "By welcoming new immigrants to our city like we did 100 years ago, we are bringing it back to life."

Mayor Jurczynski and a Guyanese visitor

Adapted from *Newsday*

12 READ B

Duc Hoang is a Vietnamese refugee. He wrote this letter to the man who helped Hoang's family move to the United States. In his letter Hoang explains how he is working to rebuild the lives of his fellow refugees, his community, and his city.

Argyle Street, Chicago

Dear Len,

I hope this letter finds you and your family well. I'm doing fine and so are Giang and the kids.

Sorry I haven't written in a while. I've been very busy. You probably remember that I'm no longer a student. I'm a social worker[1] for an immigrant organization. I try to help Vietnamese refugees, like me, rebuild their lives. The work is very rewarding. In just three years wonderful things have happened in our community.

[1] **social worker:** someone who helps others get social services (job training, health care, etc.)

When I first started my job, I went out on Argyle Street every day and interviewed refugees about their needs. People said they wanted good jobs and
10 affordable housing—they had little money and even low rents were too high for them. They worried about crime and had a hard time understanding American laws and customs. My co-workers and I came up with an idea to solve many of the problems. We got some money from a charity group and opened a community center. Starting with one staff member, two tables, and some chairs, the center grew and grew. Now
15 there are classes for learning English, classes about American culture, and special programs for youth and women. One of the most popular programs—Economic Development—teaches refugees how to do business in the United States. Several graduates are now entrepreneurs!

Do you remember when I wrote that our neighborhood was very dangerous?
20 Gangs used to hang out in the abandoned buildings[2] and there was a lot of crime. It was unsafe, but we stayed because the rents were low. One of my first jobs was to help organize a neighborhood watch system. Now everyone in the neighborhood looks out for everyone else. After a couple of neighbors helped the police catch some robbers, the crime rate went down. Next, we convinced a few landlords to rent their
25 abandoned stores to refugees at a low cost. That way the refugees could open markets and small businesses. We explained that the area would develop and grow, and the gangs would lose their hangouts.[3]

Our neighborhood has become a safe, interesting part of the city that people like to visit. More than 50 Vietnamese family-owned businesses thrive on Argyle Street,
30 but it's also very international. There are stores owned by Lao, Chinese, and Ethiopians. We have Thai, Indian, and Mexican restaurants, and even a McDonald's. Newspaper reporters come to our street to write articles praising the way Vietnamese refugees revitalized[4] the area and turned it into a beautiful place. People now call Argyle Street "Little Saigon."
35 Since I came to the Unites States, I have worked for my community. Like you, my goal is to help people. I tell my kids "it's important to share even if you have only a little to offer."

Once again I must thank you for helping my family get to the United States. I can never repay your kindness.
40

Most sincerely,
Duc Hoang

---

[2] **abandoned building:** a place that is left empty after businesses or families move out
[3] **hangout:** a place in the community where people meet
[4] **revitalize:** to bring back to life or improve

13 SHARE WHAT YOU LEARNED

A. Work with a partner who read the same text.

1. Read the focus questions for your article in the chart below.

2. Discuss the questions and write your answers.

Focus Questions for Text A
1. Why did Ramesh Doodnauth move to Schenectady?
2. What did he and other Guyanese do to help Schenectady?
3. Why is Ramesh's community a better place now?
4. What does the quote at the end of the article mean?

Focus Questions for Text B
1. Why did Duc Hoang move to the United States?
2. What did he and other social workers do to help Vietnamese refugees?
3. Why is Duc's community a better place now?
4. What does the quote toward the end of the letter mean?

B. With your partner, find a pair who read a different text and form a team.

1. Share the topic of your text with your teammates.

2. Take turns sharing the answers to the focus questions.

3. Add any other information from the article that you remember.

14 SHARE WHAT YOU THINK

Discuss these questions with your teammates. Then share your answers with the class.

1. Imagine you lived in Schenectady in the 1990s. The Guyanese haven't moved there yet. Are you happy with your community? Why or why not?

2. Imagine you have moved into a community similar to the one Duc describes. There is crime and there are few job opportunities. Schools are crowded and there aren't many parks. Which problem will you fix first? Why?

3. In cities there are often neighborhoods, such as Chinatown or Little Mexico, where most of the people are from the same ethnic group. What effect does this have on a city? What effect does it have on the immigrants who move into those neighborhoods?

Interview

Read the questions and think about your answers. Then interview a partner. With your partner, decide what common goals hold your class together.

1. What are the common goals that hold your family together?

2. What are the common goals that hold people living in your community together?

Chart

A. Work in a small group. Think of positive, negative, and interesting aspects of immigrating to another country. Look at the statements in the chart. Write two or more ideas in each section of the chart.

IMMIGRATING TO ANOTHER COUNTRY		
Positive	**Negative**	**Interesting**
have new job opportunities	leave friends and family	learn about a new culture

B. Use your group's chart to discuss these questions with your classmates.

1. What do you think is most difficult about immigrating?

2. What do you think is the greatest advantage of immigrating?

Write

A. Think about the immigration experience of someone you know or have read about. If you are an immigrant, you can think about your own experiences.

B. Write a paragraph that answers some or all of the following questions.

- Who is the immigrant that you will describe?
- Why did the person immigrate? Where did he or she go?
- What are some good things that happened in the new country?
- What are some difficulties the person experienced?
- Is he or she happy to be in a different country? Why or why not?

Unit 2

Getting Along

In this unit you will:

● read about getting along in a diverse society
● learn more previewing strategies

HOW DOES DIVERSITY AFFECT YOU?

A. The artist Norman Rockwell titled this work "The Golden Rule." The Golden Rule says that people should treat others the way they want to be treated. Why did Rockwell choose that title? Share your thoughts with your classmates.

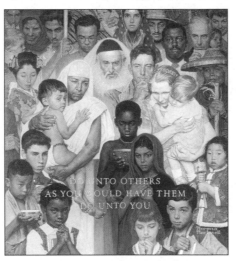

The Golden Rule by Norman Rockwell

B. Think about these statements. Do you agree or disagree? Discuss your answers with a partner. Share your ideas with your classmates.

1. College students should have to study different cultures in order to graduate.

2. Workers need to learn how to work with people from different cultures.

3. It's good for a school, a workplace, or a country to have people from different cultures or backgrounds.

17

A. Look around your classroom. Think about the ways in which the members of your class are the same or different. Circle *yes* or *no* in the columns on the right.

Do all your classmates speak the same . . .		
1. language?	YES	NO
Are all your classmates the same . . .		
2. gender?	YES	NO
3. age?	YES	NO
Do all your classmates have the same . . .		
4. ethnic background?	YES	NO
5. marital status?	YES	NO

B. Use the information in the chart to discuss these questions with a partner. Share your answers with your classmates.

1. In which ways is your class most diverse? least diverse?

2. How does diversity or lack of diversity affect your classroom?

C. Read the following paragraph, paying attention to the underlined words. Then guess which word or phrase is the best choice for each sentence below. Check your guesses after you read the article on pages 20–21.

> *Many people in the United States* <u>respect</u> *and value diversity. They appreciate the* <u>benefits</u> *of living in a diverse society where they can learn from each other. They* <u>recognize</u> *that no one person is exactly like another person. They understand that individuals* <u>differ</u> *in many ways. American children are taught that it's wrong to* <u>prevent</u> *someone from having the same opportunities as others have, just because that person is different. That type of discrimination and* <u>prejudice</u> *is against the law in the United States.*

1. When you respect people, you have a (low/high) opinion of them.

2. Benefits are the (positive/negative) effects of a situation.

3. When you recognize something as true, you (know/don't know) that it's true.

4. People who differ (are/aren't) the same.

5. When you prevent something you (stop/don't stop) it.

6. Prejudice is an opinion about a person or group that (is/isn't) based on facts.

2 BUILDING READING SKILLS: Previewing Comprehension Questions

Comprehension questions often follow a text to help you check how well you understood the material. You can also preview these questions *before* you read the text to help you pay attention to important ideas and details. Then as you read, look for the answers and mark them with a highlighter, underline them, or make notes in the margins.

Practice Previewing Comprehension Questions

A. Preview the questions that follow the paragraph below. Then, as you read the paragraph, look for the answers and highlight them. Compare answers with your classmates.

> *Diversity on college campuses is growing. Colleges recognize that differences among people help create a more interesting environment. They also know that, unfortunately, prejudice, or the hatred of certain groups, can occur when the student population is diverse. Several organizations such as Stop the Hate offer information and programs about how to prevent prejudice. They help students speak out against prejudice on campus.*

1. Why is diversity good for the college environment?
2. What problem sometimes comes with diversity?
3. What is Stop the Hate?
4. What does Stop the Hate help students do?

B. Preview the question that follows the paragraph. Then read the paragraph and note in the margin where you found the answer.

> *The American workforce is very diverse. It can be hard for workers from different backgrounds to get along if they don't understand each other. Many U.S. companies now offer diversity training to their*
> #1 *employees. These classes describe the values and traditions of different cultures. They also examine different work styles and help workers improve their communication skills. Diversity training helps employees work together more successfully.*

What are three things workers learn in diversity training?

USE YOUR READING SKILLS

A. **Preview the key elements of the article below. Then work with a partner to complete these statements.**

1. From the title and introductory material, I know this article is about . . .

2. Based on my preview of the headings, I predict I will learn . . .

B. **Preview the first three questions on page 22. Then, as you read the article, either highlight the answers to the questions or note in the margins where you found them.**

3 READ

This article from a sociology textbook describes some of the ways the United States is managing its great diversity.

Diversity: It Makes All the Difference!

All Kinds of Differences

Almost every discussion about U.S. society today includes the idea of diversity—the many ways people differ from each other. Odette Pollar, an expert on the topic, and author of *Dynamics of Diversity*, says, "This
5 definition may seem simple. But think for a moment how many kinds of differences there are, and in how many different ways they can be combined! Together, these differences are important in shaping us as individuals."

Pollar names all kinds of differences among people. We vary in gender, age, ethnic background, race, marital status, religion, physical ability, mental
10 ability, language skills, and life experience. We think, learn, and work differently. Not surprisingly, we also have different ideas about relationships, family, and politics.

Many Americans recognize the benefits of a diverse society. They understand that a variety of backgrounds, points of view,[1] and talents make a
15 society richer and more interesting. However, such differences also create challenges.[2] Sometimes people see each other as different without trying to understand why. Throughout U.S. history, there are examples of how this lack of understanding has led to prejudice and discrimination. For this reason, government, businesses, and schools keep working hard to prevent
20 such discrimination from happening.

Diversity Laws

The U.S. government has made laws to make sure that peoples' differences will not prevent them from getting a job, getting an education, or

---

[1] **point of view:** an opinion
[2] **challenge:** a difficult or problematic situation

participating in society. For example, the Civil Rights Act of 1964 makes it
illegal to discriminate against a person on the basis of race, color, religion,
gender, or national origin. The law names three main areas in which
discrimination is not allowed: employment; services such as schools, stores,
restaurants, and hotels; and government programs. According to Title IX of
the Education Amendments of 1972, it's illegal to discriminate on the basis of
gender in all educational programs that receive money from the government.
This law requires that males and females have equal opportunity to develop
their skills and talents. As a result of Title IX, today many more girls and
women participate in school sports.

Laws have done a great deal to protect a person's rights. However, they
don't do much to help the average person deal with the everyday challenges
that go along with diversity. Support of this kind is taking place in American
schools and businesses.

Diversity Education

Colleges and universities throughout the United States are teaching courses
in diversity. First, students learn about the history and traditions of various
ethnic groups. Then they examine their own culture in relation to the ones
they have studied. Many colleges require students to take these courses before
they can graduate, and most Americans think this is a good idea. Recently the
Ford Foundation funded[3] a poll on diversity in higher education. Two-thirds
of the participants in the poll said that it's important for colleges to prepare
students to live in a diverse society.

Business leaders know that diversity is an asset[4] in a company, and many
of them provide diversity training for their employees. The purpose is to
create a workplace where everyone understands, respects, and values the
differences of others. In the classes, employees identify and discuss different
work styles. They learn how to appreciate each other's strengths and work
together better.

The Power of One Person

When Odette Pollar gives diversity training courses, she tells people,
"Think of a person as a pebble tossed into a lake. The pebble may be small,
but the ripples it creates get bigger and bigger until they splash onto the
shore, sometimes miles away." As each person takes a small step toward
accepting others, prejudice will fade away.[5] As time goes on, more and more
people will begin to realize that the diversity of its society is one of America's
greatest natural resources.

---

[3] **fund:** to give money for a project
[4] **asset:** something useful, an advantage
[5] **fade away:** to go away slowly

4 PROCESS WHAT YOU READ

A. Answer these questions. Look back at the article on pages 20–21 to check your answers.

1. What is diversity?

2. What are three ways in which people are different?

3. What are the benefits of a diverse society?

4. What can happen when people don't understand each other's differences?

5. How does the U.S. government fight discrimination?

6. What do college students learn in a diversity course?

7. What did the Ford Foundation poll show?

8. What is the purpose of diversity training in business?

B. Choose the idea under each heading that does not appear in the article on pages 20–21. Look back at the article to check your answers.

1. All Kinds of Differences

   a. Differences shape us as individuals.
   b. Few people value diversity.
   c. Differences can create challenges.

2. Diversity Laws

   a. Laws help people with the everyday challenges of diversity.
   b. Laws protect individual's rights.
   c. Laws protect people against discrimination.

3. Diversity Education

   a. Colleges and businesses have classes on diversity.
   b. Studying diversity helps people understand each other better.
   c. Diversity education creates challenges for society.

4. The Power of One Person

   a. A small action can have a big effect.
   b. One person's actions create prejudice.
   c. Understanding others can make prejudice fade away.

C. Think about these questions. Then discuss them with your classmates.

1. The article on pages 20–21 mentions that many colleges and businesses are teaching diversity courses. Imagine you are teaching a diversity course. What topics will you cover?

2. Water and trees are examples of common natural resources. The article calls diversity a natural resource. Do you agree? Why or why not?

5 WORK WITH THE VOCABULARY

A. Complete each sentence below with the correct word from the word family in the box.

Verb: differ	*Noun:* differences	*Adverb:* differently	*Adjective:* different

1. There are all kinds of ___differences___ among people.

2. For example, they can _____ in gender, age, and ethnic background.

3. They may also have _____ language skills or life experiences.

4. It's no surprise that people often think and act _____.

B. Write the verb forms of the nouns below. Look back at the article on pages 20–21 to help you. Check answers with a partner.

creation ___create___   discussion _____

participation _____   prevention _____

discrimination _____   protection _____

C. Use the verb forms you wrote in part B to complete these sentences. Look back at the article to check your answers.

1. Diversity can _____ challenges for society.

2. People's differences should not _____ them from participating in society.

3. Laws have done a great deal to _____ a person's rights.

4. It's illegal to _____ against a person on the basis of race, color, religion, gender, or national origin.

5. As a result of Title IX, many more girls and women _____ in school sports.

6. In diversity training, employees _____ different work styles.

D. Cross out the word that does not belong in each word set.

1. benefit   ~~problem~~   advantage   improvement
2. respect   honor   value   dislike
3. prejudice   hate   diversity   discrimination
4. recognize   know   understand   forget

A. Imagine that you have an assignment to write a paper about yourself. Put a check (✓) next to the three items of information that would most help someone understand who you are. Then share that information with a partner.

___ my birthplace   ___ my home town

___ my birth date   ___ my hobbies

___ my ethnic background   ___ my family

___ my education   ___ my friends' opinions of me

___ my marital status   ___ other _____

B. Read the beginning of Langston Hughes's poem "Theme for English B" below. Then discuss the questions that follow with your classmates.

> The instructor said,
>
>> Go home and write
>> a page tonight,
>> And let that page come out of you—
>> Then, it will be true.

1. What assignment does the instructor give?

2. Why will the paper be true?

3. The words "write" and "tonight" rhyme. What other words in this part of the poem rhyme?

4. Do you think it is easier to read a poem or a newspaper article? Why?

USE YOUR READING SKILLS

A. Preview the key elements of the poem on page 25. Then answer these questions. As you read the poem, check your answers.

1. Who is the author? What did you know about him before you previewed the poem?

2. What is the topic of the poem? What do you already know about the topic?

3. What else do you predict you will learn about Hughes in the poem?

B. Preview the questions in exercise A on page 26. Highlight the answers as you read the poem.

Langston Hughes grew up in the South of the U.S. and went to college in the North. In this poem, Hughes writes about his life as a young African American college student in New York City.

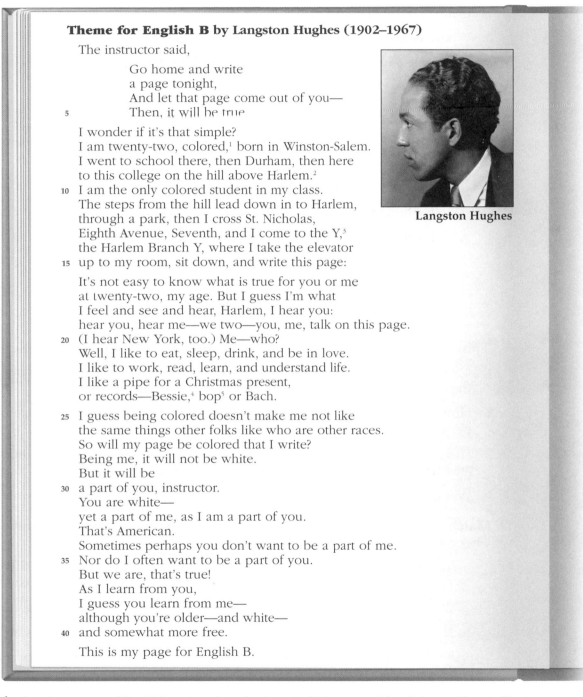

Theme for English B by Langston Hughes (1902–1967)

The instructor said,

    Go home and write
    a page tonight,
    And let that page come out of you—
5   Then, it will be true.

I wonder if it's that simple?
I am twenty-two, colored,[1] born in Winston-Salem.
I went to school there, then Durham, then here
to this college on the hill above Harlem.[2]
10 I am the only colored student in my class.
The steps from the hill lead down in to Harlem,
through a park, then I cross St. Nicholas,
Eighth Avenue, Seventh, and I come to the Y,[3]
the Harlem Branch Y, where I take the elevator
15 up to my room, sit down, and write this page:

It's not easy to know what is true for you or me
at twenty-two, my age. But I guess I'm what
I feel and see and hear, Harlem, I hear you:
hear you, hear me—we two—you, me, talk on this page.
20 (I hear New York, too.) Me—who?
Well, I like to eat, sleep, drink, and be in love.
I like to work, read, learn, and understand life.
I like a pipe for a Christmas present,
or records—Bessie,[4] bop[5] or Bach.

25 I guess being colored doesn't make me not like
the same things other folks like who are other races.
So will my page be colored that I write?
Being me, it will not be white.
But it will be
30 a part of you, instructor.
You are white—
yet a part of me, as I am a part of you.
That's American.
Sometimes perhaps you don't want to be a part of me.
35 Nor do I often want to be a part of you.
But we are, that's true!
As I learn from you,
I guess you learn from me—
although you're older—and white—
40 and somewhat more free.

This is my page for English B.

Langston Hughes

---

[1] **colored:** a term used for African Americans in the early 20th century. Now it is considered offensive.
[2] **Harlem:** a part of New York City where most of the residents were African Americans
[3] **Y:** Young Men's Christian Association (YMCA), which often rents rooms at low cost
[4] **Bessie Smith:** a famous Jazz singer
[5] **bop:** short for "bebop," a style of music

A. Answer the questions. Discuss your answers with a partner. Look back at the poem to check your answers.

1. Is the English class diverse?

2. Where was Hughes born? Where did he go to school?

3. How does Hughes walk home from the college?

4. Where does Hughes live?

5. What are three things Hughes likes to do?

B. Number the events in the order that they happen. Look back at the poem to check your answers.

____ Hughes writes that the things he likes are the same as what other people like.

____ He writes about where he lives.

____ He recognizes that everyone is a part of everyone else.

____ He walks to his room in Harlem and sits down to write the poem.

__1__ He gets a writing assignment.

____ He writes about what he likes to do.

C. Think about these questions. Share your answers with your classmates.

1. Look at questions 1–5 in Exercise A above. Why does Hughes talk about each of these things in the poem?

2. How do you think Langston Hughes feels about being the only African-American person in the class?

3. How do you think Hughes feels about having a white instructor? Imagine he has an African American instructor. How do you think he feels?

4. What do you think Langston Hughes means when he says "That's American"?

D. Match phrases from the poem with the statements that have a similar meaning. Check your answers with a partner.

____ 1. "let that page come out of you"

____ 2. "it will be true"

____ 3. "Harlem . . . you, me, talk on this page."

____ 4. "You are white —
yet a part of me, as I am a part of you."

a. Although we are different, we have an effect on each other.

b. It will be honest and real.

c. Write from your heart.

d. Where I live is a part of me.

A. Read the paragraph about stereotypes. Then use the information to decide whether the statements in the chart are facts or stereotypes. Check (✓) the correct boxes.

> *Stereotypes*
>
> *Sometimes people form opinions about groups of other people and make overly simple, general statements about them. These statements are called stereotypes. They aren't true and they aren't based on facts. Stereotyping people often causes discrimination.*

Statement	Fact	Stereotype
1. Some people are good drivers.	✓	
2. Women are talkative.		
3. Many college students play sports.		
4. Bankers think about money all the time		
5. Men don't ask for directions.		

B. Think about these questions. Then discuss your answers with a partner. Share your ideas with your classmates.

1. How do stereotypes affect people's lives?

2. How can stereotyping cause discrimination?

C. Put a check (✓) next to the words you know. Ask your classmates for the meanings of the words you don't know. Look up the words no one knows in a dictionary.

____ ashamed   ____ extraordinary   ____ impact   ____ offensive

____ oppose   ____ get rid of   ____ slavery   ____ tension

D. Preview the key elements of the two texts on pages 28–30. Then answer these questions.

1. What is the topic of text A?

2. What is the topic of text B?

E. Choose one text to read, and preview the focus questions for your article on page 31. Then answer these questions.

1. What is the title of your text?

2. What do you already know about the topic?

3. Based on the focus questions, what do you predict you will learn?

People from different communities often find it difficult to understand each other. This newspaper article discusses one of the problems Native Americans face.

Fighting Braves

Across the United States, sports fans cheer for the Braves, the Indians, and the Chiefs.[1] Who are they cheering for? They're shouting for
5 their teams, who have named themselves after Native Americans. Often the mascot, the symbol of the team, is a Native
10 American in a feathered headdress. Sometimes it's a cartoon image of a Native American with red skin and a silly look in his eye.
15 There are thousands of high schools, dozens of colleges and universities, and a handful of professional teams that use these names and symbols. Some people say that this practice
20 celebrates the strength and courage of the Native American people and encourages interest in Native American culture. However, many Native Americans do not agree.

25 The Native American community believes that the use of these names and symbols by sports teams encourages[2] stereotyping and discrimination. Cornel D. Pewewardy,
30 Assistant Professor at the University of Kansas, believes that many young Indigenous People[3] feel ashamed, or embarrassed, about who they are when they see their cultural
35 symbols used as mascots. The U.S. Commission on Civil Rights agrees that using these symbols "teaches all students that
40 stereotyping of minority groups is acceptable, a dangerous lesson in a diverse society." According to the Commission, teams that
45 continue to use Native American names and symbols are not listening to and respecting the wishes of native groups. However, sports fans value their teams' traditions and
50 many don't want to change the names they love.

In the town of Tomales, California, people are passionate[4] about their high school team, the Braves. When
55 the student council suggested a name change, people had strong opinions both ways. "It was a big controversy in this small town," says Kerri Azevedo, student body president
60 of Tomales High School. "Many

---

[1] **Braves, Indians, Chiefs:** all terms for Native Americans: a *brave* is a warrior, or soldier; a *chief* is a leader; *Indian* is another word for Native American.
[2] **encourage:** to make something happen more easily
[3] **Indigenous People:** the first people in a place, e.g., Native Americans in America, Aborigines in Australia
[4] **passionate:** showing strong feeling

people were against it, while many people agreed with it." The Native Americans in the community supported the student council, but the people who opposed the name change spoke loudly. "There were banners saying 'Save the Braves' put up all around the town," reports Azevedo. Finally, as a compromise[5] the students and the school board voted to keep the name but change the mascot. "The students feel our team is as courageous as braves, so we want to keep the name," says Kerri. "We just want to get rid of all the symbols that might be offensive to Native Americans. We will keep the colors of red, black, and white but change our symbol to a hawk."

Stereotypes of all kinds are a difficult problem. People often don't realize their impact. The U.S. Commission on Civil Rights believes that stereotypes are part of the reason for the extremely low numbers of Native American high school and college graduates. According to the Commission, schools have a responsibility to educate their students by representing all cultures and peoples truthfully. They should provide education about current Native American issues and the rich cultural traditions of the many Native American groups in the United States. The Commission believes that getting rid of stereotypes will benefit not only Native Americans but all Americans.

[5] **compromise:** an agreement that results when each side accepts part of what it originally wanted

11 READ B

Sharing a common interest can often bring different groups together. This web page describes how two groups gained friendship and understanding through song.

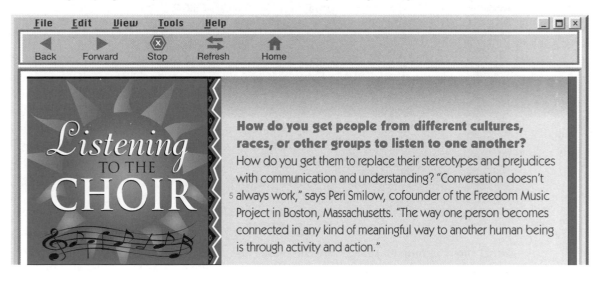

File   Edit   View   Tools   Help

Back   Forward   Stop   Refresh   Home

Listening TO THE CHOIR

How do you get people from different cultures, races, or other groups to listen to one another? How do you get them to replace their stereotypes and prejudices with communication and understanding? "Conversation doesn't always work," says Peri Smilow, cofounder of the Freedom Music Project in Boston, Massachusetts. "The way one person becomes connected in any kind of meaningful way to another human being is through activity and action."

Smilow put her beliefs to work by helping
to form a singing group with nine African
American teenagers and nine Jewish American
teenagers. "The goal of our project was to
bring together people from two different
backgrounds who shared a common interest.
Each teen loved singing and would do
anything to hang out and sing." Another goal of
the project was to improve relations between
African Americans and Jewish Americans in
the area. "We believed," says Smilow, "that the
music would help the young people find a
way to understand each other."

Smilow got the idea for the project when
she attended an African American–Jewish
Passover Seder in Boston in 1997. The Passover
Seder is a religious feast, a special meal during
which Jewish people remember and
celebrate their freedom from slavery. African
Americans have also been slaves, and to honor
their shared experience of freedom from
slavery, every year about 1,000 African
Americans and Jewish people celebrate
Passover together. In 1997 a youth gospel
choir[1] was invited to sing at the dinner. The
director of the choir, LeRoix Hampton, taught
the teens a well-known Jewish folk song in
Hebrew. According to Smilow, "The result was
extraordinary—Jewish and African American
audience members alike jumped to their feet
to applaud and sing with the choir. The group
was a hit!"

After that performance, Hampton and
Smilow decided to form a new group of
African American and Jewish singers. The
choir, called the Freedom Music Project, sings
freedom songs from the Civil Rights movement[2]
and from the Passover celebration. Kevin
Vaydeak, one of the singers, says, "The
Passover message, 'We were slaves and now
we're free,' means just as much to us as
African Americans, as to the Jews." Hampton
makes sure the teens understand what they
are singing, so that it will be a meaningful
experience for both singers and listeners.
"You've got to feel your singing. It's got to be
from the heart," says Hampton.

When the choir first formed, not everything
went smoothly. Each group had to learn music
from the other group's traditions. Learning such
unfamiliar music was difficult, and this caused
some tension. Also, the teens had different
ways of learning. Some learned their parts by
reading sheet music, and some learned by ear.
"The point of the Freedom Music Project was
to learn to work through those difficulties,"
said Smilow. One of the teenagers, Noam
Katz, said "People had to find a way to work
things out, so we encouraged each other and
joked with each other."

When Hampton and Smilow started the
singing group, they hoped the music would
be the first step on the path toward mutual[3]
understanding and friendship. "When I was a
child I learned from my parents that the
smallest action can lead to big change," says
Peri Smilow. "With groups like this we're going
to change the world."

[1] **gospel choir:** a group that sings Christian music, first sung by African Americans in the southern U.S.
[2] **Civil Rights movement:** political action beginning in the 1950s with the goal of equal rights for all races
[3] **mutual:** shared by two or more people

12 SHARE WHAT YOU LEARNED

A. Work with a partner who read the same article.

1. Read the focus questions for your article in the chart below.

2. Discuss the questions and write the answers.

FOCUS QUESTIONS FOR TEXT A
1. Why do sports teams name themselves after Native Americans?
2. Why do Native Americans dislike the use of their names and symbols by teams?
3. What did the Tomales School Board decide to do? Do you think Native Americans were happy about the decision?
4. Why is it difficult to solve the conflict between Native Americans and sports teams that want to use Native American names and symbols?

FOCUS QUESTIONS FOR TEXT B
1. Why did Hampton and Smilow form the Freedom Music Project?
2. Why are the freedom songs meaningful to all the singers?
3. What were some of the difficulties the choir members had?
4. What helped the young people communicate better with each other?

B. With your partner, find a pair who read a different text and form a team.

1. Share the topic of your text with your teammates.

2. Take turns sharing the answers to the focus questions.

3. Add any other information from the text that you remember.

13 SHARE WHAT YOU THINK

Discuss these questions with your teammates. Then share your answers with the class.

1. What are some ways people can learn to get along with each other?

2. What do you think are the main causes of misunderstandings between people? Why?

3. What kinds of things have you done to help you learn about other people or cultures? What can you do to learn more?

14 REFLECT ON WHAT YOU READ IN THIS UNIT

Interview

Read the quote and think about the questions. Then interview a partner. With your partner, decide whether diversity is the great problem or promise of our time.

> *"As our nation grows more diverse . . . our diversity will either be the great problem or the great promise of the 21st century."*
>
> —Bill Clinton, 42nd President of the United States

1. What problems may result from the growing diversity of the United States?

2. What positive results, or great promise, could an increase in diversity bring?

Chart and Write

A. Think about U.S. culture and another culture. Write a list of items that represent each culture. Using your lists, follow the model to create a Venn diagram. Put items that are common to both cultures in the "Both" section.

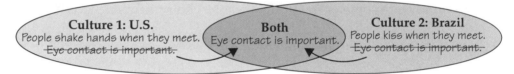

Culture 1: U.S.
People shake hands when they meet.
~~Eye contact is important.~~

Both
Eye contact is important.

Culture 2: Brazil
People kiss when they meet.
~~Eye contact is important.~~

15 REFLECT ON YOUR READING STRATEGIES

Read the questions in the chart and check the answers that best describe your use of the reading strategies. Then with your classmates, discuss which strategies are the most helpful.

Strategy	How often do you use this strategy outside of this class?			How helpful is this strategy?		
	Always	Sometimes	Never	Very	A little	Not
Previewing the title, author, and source						
Previewing the illustrations and headings						
Previewing questions						
Identifying what you already know about a topic						
Predicting what you will learn from a text						

Unit 3

Looking at Looks

In this unit you will:

- read about the role of appearance in the U.S.
- learn how to scan a text
- learn a strategy for reading faster

HOW IMPORTANT IS APPEARANCE?

A. Talk about the cartoon below with your classmates. Decide which of the following sentences best describes the young woman in the cartoon.

"Looking good! Feeling great! And soon to be famous!"

1. She has to check her appearance in the mirror before she can feel good.

2. She feels so confident about her appearance that she thinks she can do anything.

3. She's having a really good day so she looks good.

B. Think about these questions. Discuss your answers with a partner. Then share your ideas with your classmates.

1. Is it more important to look good or to feel good? Why?

2. Is physical appearance important for success? Why or why not?

3. Do most people like their looks? Explain.

A. Take the quiz and compare answers with a partner.

First Impressions Quiz

1. What's the most important thing to do when you first meet someone?

a. smile   b. shake hands   c. say "hello"

2. What do people think about most when they first meet you?

a. how you speak   b. how you look   c. how you act

3. How long does it take for someone to decide what kind of person you are?

a. 1 hour   b. 10 minutes   c. 30 seconds

B. Read the sentences below. Guess which word or phrase has a meaning similar to the underlined words. Highlight your guesses and check them after you read the article on pages 36–37.

1. Many people are <u>satisfied</u> with their appearance. They're happy with the way they look.

2. However, <u>dissatisfaction</u> with body image is a problem for people of all ages. This unhappiness often makes them want to change their faces or bodies.

3. <u>Cosmetic surgery</u> can make a person look different. This medical treatment can change the shape of the face or body.

4. A change in appearance can often increase a person's <u>self-esteem</u>. For example, a new haircut may improve how someone feels about himself or herself.

5. Magazine ads try to <u>convince people</u> to buy beauty products. They try to make people believe that the products will make them more attractive.

6. These ads depend on people's <u>vanity</u>. Advertisers know that some people spend too much time thinking about their appearance.

7. Many people <u>judge</u> others just by looking at them. For example, they might form an opinion about someone based only on the person's clothing.

8. Some people think it's easy to tell a person's <u>character</u>. They decide that someone has good or bad qualities based only on the person's looks.

> **Scanning** means looking for specific information without reading a whole text. When you scan, you move your eyes quickly down the page to look for certain words or signals (capital letters, numbers, symbols, etc.) that will lead you to the information you want. Sometimes important words will be **boldfaced**, *italicized*, or underlined. There may also be a bullet (•) next to a key idea or fact.

Read the information in the chart.

To find this information,	scan for this signal.
a name of a person or place	capital letters (ABC)
a date, time, address, or phone number	numbers
a price	$, numbers
a percent	%, numbers
a website	www.
an e-mail address	@
something someone said	" " (quotation marks)
a key idea or fact	• (bullet)

Practice Scanning

Scan the ad below for the following information. Highlight the information you find and circle the signal you used to find it. Compare answers with a partner.

1. doctor's name
2. website
3. doctor's advice
4. types of surgery
5. e-mail address
6. phone in New Orleans

Look Years Younger ~ Improve Your Image with Cosmetic Surgery

Lindsay Allison, M.D., a cosmetic surgeon for over 15 years, completed her training at the University of Texas, and received her certification from the American Board of Cosmetic Surgery in 1990. Dr. Allison is also on the list of *Best Doctors in Southern Louisiana*. Her specialties include:

- Surgery of the Face, Eyes, Nose and Ears
- Wrinkle Removal
- Tattoo Removal

Dr. Allison offers a line of skin care products that improve the healing process by 50%. Dr. Allison says, "Use my creams and lotions. Your skin will get the important vitamins it needs: A, B, D, E, and K."

Thinking about cosmetic surgery? Take a look at our website: www.yearsyounger.com. Feel free to e-mail us at allison@yearsyounger.com, or call us in Baton Rouge at 866-555-1415 or in New Orleans at 504-555-1112.

Use Your Reading Skills

A. Preview the article below. Then complete these statements. Check your answers as you read the article.

1. From my preview, I know that this article is about . . .

2. Based on my preview, I predict I will learn . . .

B. Scan the article below for the following information:

1. What is the name of a popular magazine? _____ "Family Circle"

2. How many people answered a questionnaire about their looks?

    _____

3. How many people said they were very satisfied with the way they look?

    _____

4. How many men wanted to have cosmetic surgery? _____

5. Who said, "Dissatisfaction with body image is very common in America"?

    _____

6. What percent of first impressions are based on what people say?

    _____

C. Preview the questions in exercise A on page 38. As you read the article, highlight the answers or note in the margins where you found them.

3 READ

In the United States there is great interest in personal appearance. This psychology magazine article explains why.

The U.S. Focus on Image

Americans care a great deal about how they look. Open any newspaper or magazine, listen to any radio station, or watch TV.
5 You'll see and hear advertisements that tell people to lose weight, whiten their teeth, or have cosmetic surgery. These ads try to convince people to do something to improve
10 their looks. Is it all just a matter of vanity, or is it important to take care of your appearance?

The popular magazine *Family Circle* asked 432 men and women
15 how they felt about themselves. While 13% were very satisfied with their looks, 63% were only partly satisfied. More than 50% of the women and 23% of the men
20 wanted to have cosmetic surgery. Only 15% of women thought they were very overweight, but two-thirds of the women wanted to lose some weight. "Dissatisfaction

with body image is very common in America," says Dr. David Sarwer, Assistant Professor of Psychology at the University of Pennsylvania School of Medicine. "Many people hope that surgery will help them feel better about their appearance, which in turn may help them have better self-esteem."

But are looks really that important? Research shows that they are. Fifty-five percent of first impressions are based on appearance, 38% are based on body language[1] and only 7% are based on what you say. People really are forming opinions by looking at your clothes, your hair, your skin, and your size, and they're doing it all in 30 seconds!

In one study, researchers showed some students photographs of different people and told stories about each one. Then they asked the students to judge the behavior and character of the people they saw. This is one story the students heard: "This woman is a cashier at a market. The owners think she stole some money from the store. For several days, money was missing from her cash register. Yesterday she came to work with an expensive new purse, which she couldn't afford. Should she be fired for stealing?"

Most of the students who heard this story and saw a photo of an unattractive woman thought the woman should be fired. However, when the researchers told the same story to another group of students and showed a photo of an attractive woman, most of them responded differently. They said that the woman didn't steal the money and shouldn't be fired.

Time after time, in situation after situation, appearance influenced[2] how students felt about a person's character. In almost all cases, attractive people got a positive response. Most students thought attractive people would be better romantic partners, would make better doctors, and would be better employees than less attractive people.

Appearance clearly plays an important role in the lives of many Americans, but vanity may not be the main reason why. The research shows that people's concern with appearance may result from a desire to make a positive impression on others. If society feels more positive about someone, his or her chances of success in society are greater. After all, doesn't everybody want to succeed?

[1] **body language:** communication of feelings through movement, gesture, body position, etc.
[2] **influence:** to have an effect on something or somebody

4 PROCESS WHAT YOU READ

A. Answer the questions. Discuss your answers with a partner. Look back at the article to check your answers.

1. What role does advertising play in Americans' focus on image?

2. Why do people have cosmetic surgery?

3. According to research, what do people pay attention to when they first meet someone or judge someone's character?

4. Name three reasons why people in the United States think appearance is important.

B. Look back at the quiz on page 34. Answer the questions again using the information from the article.

C. Think about these questions. Discuss them with your classmates.

1. Do you think you can tell a person's character from a his or her looks? Why or why not?

2. Is your appearance or the appearance of others important to you on the job or in your personal life? Why or why not?

5 WORK WITH THE VOCABULARY

Choose the correct word to complete each sentence below. Look back at the article to check your answers. Then work with a partner to write a new sentence using each word.

a. appearance	b. character	c. convince
d. judge	e. satisfied	f. vanity

1. Some people aren't ____ when they look in the mirror.

2. Dissatisfaction with ____ is common among people who worry about their looks.

3. Advertisers try to ____ people that certain products will make them look better.

4. One reason people think so much about their looks is ____ .

5. People also worry about their appearance because others ____ them on the way they look.

6. It's better to form opinions based on a person's behavior and ____ .

6 IMPROVING READING SPEED AND COMPREHENSION: Skipping Words You Don't Know

> **Skipping words you don't know** will help you read faster. You can usually understand the meaning of a text without reading every word.

Practice Skipping Words You Don't Know

A. Read the following paragraph quickly. Skip over the missing words (xxx). Then answer the questions below. Check your answers with a partner.

Dressing for a Job Interview, by Amanda Dailey

Appropriate dress for a job interview can be different xxxxxxxxx on the kind of job you are trying to get. Once I went on an interview for a job as a xxxxxxx artist. I wore formal clothes—a jacket and nice xxxxxx. When I arrived, all the other xxxxxxxxxx were wearing unusual clothing that xxxxxxxxx their personal, artistic style. I felt very xxx xx xxxxx and I didn't get the job. I've decided that to get a job in xxxxxxx design, I need to dress less like a business person and more like an artist.

1. What kind of job did Amanda want?

    a. salesperson   b. clothes designer   c. graphic artist

2. At the job interview, what were most of the people wearing?

    a. formal clothing   b. unusual clothing   c. winter clothing

3. How will Amanda dress at her next interview?

    a. like an artist   b. like a businessperson   c. like a student

B. Could you answer the questions without knowing every word? Why or why not? Discuss your answers with your classmates.

7 GET READY TO READ ABOUT: Business Dressing

A. Work with a partner to answer these questions.

1. What do office workers usually wear to work these days? Why?

2. Do you think employees work harder when they wear comfortable clothes? Why or why not?

B. Put a check (✓) next to the words you know. Ask your classmates for the meanings of the words you don't know. Look up the words no one knows in a dictionary.

____ appropriate   ____ casual   ____ conservative   ____ executives

____ formal   ____ flexibility   ____ productive   ____ strict

Use Your Reading Skills

A. **Preview the article below. Then answer these questions.**

1. What is the topic of this article?

2. What do you already know about the topic?

3. What do you predict you will learn from this article?

B. **Read the article quickly, skipping any words you don't know. Time your reading. Put the start time at the top and the end time at the bottom. Then answer the questions on page 42.**

8 READ

🕐 **Start time** _____

Americans wore formal business clothing to the office for most of the 20th century. However, in the 1980s casual clothing became the "in" style. This magazine article shows how ideas about what to wear to work are always changing.

Back to Business?

Dressing for work isn't as easy as it used to be. Men and women used to know what was appropriate to wear in an office: for women, a
5 jacket and a skirt, or a dress; for men, a suit or a sports coat and slacks, and of course, a tie. Then, in the 1980s, casual dress became popular. "Come to work dressed
10 casually, but not too casually," said the bosses. That was the problem. More flexibility in the dress code, or rules, made it hard to know exactly what to wear.

15 Why did the office dress code change in the first place? In the 1980s many American companies offered weekly casual or "dress down" days as a special summertime
20 treat for employees. It was fun for the workers and didn't cost the companies anything. Of course, employers also expected that more comfortable workers would
25 be more productive. That certainly seemed to be true at computer companies. When people wore khakis[1] and jeans to the office at computer companies, the
30 companies made millions of dollars. Executives in other businesses thought that casual dress might produce the same success for them.

Companies gave their
35 employees permission to wear casual clothes once a week,

[1] **khakis:** light brown, casual cotton pants

usually on Friday. By the year 2001, at least 50 percent of all U.S. companies had "casual Fridays" or other casual dress days. Even conservative companies like IBM and Morgan Stanley started casual dress days.

By the beginning of this century, some company executives started to question the casual dress codes. Some workers didn't just dress casually; they wore torn jeans, halter tops, and sandals to work. This extremely casual dressing affected morale[2] and productivity in a negative way. Some employees seemed to be thinking about the weekend instead of their work. Many executives believed that dressing down was bringing the workplace down. One person reported that every Monday he had to correct the many errors that his employees had made on the previous casual Friday.

Employers began to see a connection between clothes and attitude. Many believed that more formal dress would increase work productivity. They began to write new, strict dress codes that stated exactly what people could and could not wear. Some executives put on formal business suits even though their companies had casual dress policies. They felt that suits gave them more authority,[3] helping them be more successful in business negotiations[4] and meetings with customers. Job applicants also realized that a suit gave them an advantage in getting a job.

What will the future bring? "Americans will wear a combination of formal business and dressier casual clothes," predicts Bert Hand, chairman and CEO of Hartmarx Corporation, a producer of men's and women's clothing. "There will be casual Fridays and casual dressing during the summer, but the suit will be back." Andrea Pass, vice president of Maximum Exposure Public Relations, agrees. "Women will dress more formally," says Pass. "The look will get back to business."

[2] **morale:** the attitude of a group of people
[3] **authority:** power
[4] **negotiation:** a discussion in which people try to agree on something

 **End time** _____

9 PROCESS WHAT YOU READ

A. **Mark the answers true (T) or false (F) without looking back at the article. Then check your answers on page 130. Follow the instructions for recording your comprehension score and reading speed on the inside back cover.**

____ 1. Before 1980 a suit was not appropriate clothing for men in an office.

____ 2. Some companies changed their dress codes in the 1980s.

____ 3. Some workers made mistakes or wore inappropriate clothing on casual dress days.

____ 4. Some companies made stricter dress codes because they believed more casual dress helps workers work harder.

____ 5. Some workers think wearing suits will help them be more successful.

B. **Scan the article on pages 40–41 and highlight the answers to these questions.**

1. In 2001 what percent of companies had casual dress days?

2. Which conservative companies had casual dress days?

3. What does Burt Hand predict?

10 WORK WITH THE VOCABULARY

> **Adjectives** can describe nouns.   **Adverbs** can describe verbs.
>
> He likes <u>casual</u> clothes.   He dresses <u>casually</u>.

Choose the correct form of the word in each sentence.

1. a. Employees usually like to dress (comfortable/comfortably) at work.

   b. They want to wear (comfortable/comfortably) clothing.

2. a. Sometimes dressing casually helps workers be more (productive/productively).

   b. In other situations it causes people to work less (productive/productively).

3. a. It's important to dress (appropriate/appropriately) for work.

   b. (Appropriate/Appropriately) clothing helps people do a good job.

4. a. Some companies have very (conservative/conservatively) dress codes.

   b. They want their employees to dress (conservative/conservatively).

5. a. It's important to wear (formal/formally) business clothes for important meetings.

   b. Dressing (formal/formally) can give an advantage in a job interview.

A. **Look at the pictures of body art. Then answer the questions below with your classmates.**

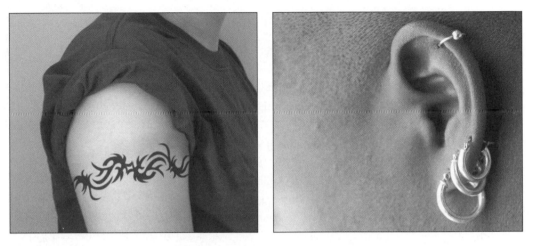

   1. What's your opinion of tattooing and piercing?

   2. Do you or your friends have body art? Why or why not?

B. **Put a check (✓) next to the words you know. Ask your classmates for the meanings of the words you don't know. Look up the words no one knows in a dictionary.**

   ___ independence   ___ infection   ___ precaution   ___ regret (v.)

   ___ risk (n.)   ___ self-expression   ___ shock (v.)   ___ trend

C. **Preview the two texts on pages 44–46. Then answer these questions.**

   1. What is the topic of text A? Will it be for or against body art?

   2. What is the topic of text B? Will it be for or against body art?

D. **Choose one text to read. Scan the text to find out how many people participated in the study on body art. Then complete these statements. Check your answers as you read the article.**

   1. The title of my article is . . .

   2. The number of people in the study on body art was . . .

   3. Complete either statement *a* or statement *b*.

      a. I predict that my article will support the argument for body art with the following reasons:

      b. I predict that my article will support the argument against body art with the following reasons:

Americans are getting tattoos and piercings in record numbers. This magazine article looks at why this form of self-expression, or body art, is becoming so popular.

Body Art

Why do so many Americans like body art? In a study of almost 500 college students, 60% of women and 42% of men had piercings on various
5 parts of their bodies. Twenty percent of the group also had tattoos. Research shows that the body art trend is growing.

"This is how I express myself,"
10 says 21-year-old Marina Harding, a graduate student from Seattle, Washington. Marina has bright green hair and piercings on her tongue, lip, nose, and eyebrow, and
15 six in each ear. "I dress this way to shock you" says the motto written on Marina's T-shirt. Marina also has eight tattoos and she wants to get more. "I love body art!" she says.

20 Experts say that people pierce and tattoo their bodies to show they are different from others, or to remember an important event in their lives. Body art also shows a
25 person's sense of fashion and may increase their status[1] in a group. Body art may make a person appear more "cool" and less traditional. Jonathan Daulton, 19, has ten

30 piercings on his face. "Honestly, I do it to be outrageous,"[2] says the computer science student at the University of Nebraska.

TV stars, movie stars, and
35 musicians are often the role models[3] for body art. Thousands of people tattoo themselves to look just like their favorite stars. Tattooing has become so popular that it's one of
40 the fastest growing service businesses in the United States.

People with piercings and tattoos may not know it but they are part of an ancient[4] tradition. According to
45 anthropologist Enid Schildkrout of the American Museum of Natural History in New York City, "There is no culture in which people do not paint, pierce, tattoo, reshape, and
50 adorn[5] their bodies." Schildkrout, who organized a museum show on body art, says, "We want people to realize that everyone, including themselves, performs some type of
55 transformation. We color our hair, wear makeup, put on clothes, have cosmetic surgery." People's reasons for changing themselves are the

[1] **status:** social position
[2] **outrageous:** very unusual and surprising
[3] **role model:** someone whom people admire and try to copy
[4] **ancient:** very, very old
[5] **adorn:** decorate

same as they have been for
60 thousands of years: to attract a
romantic partner, improve
self-esteem, show membership in
a group, and show independence.

Whatever the reasons, more and
65 more people are piercing and
tattooing themselves. They could be
rebelling[6] against their parents and
society, or trying hard to fit into their
peer groups. Since history shows us
70 that everyone adorns themselves in
one way or another, tattooing and
piercings are just one of the many
choices. What will be next?

---

[6] **rebel:** to oppose authority or people in power

13 READ B

Tattoos and piercings are popular forms of self-expression. However, doctors say there are risks involved. This newspaper article discusses those risks and how to decrease them.

A Risky Trend

For many people in the United States, the growing popularity of body
art—tattoos and piercings—is a disturbing trend. In a study of over 2,000
young people, more than 50% wanted to get a tattoo and 10% already
had one. Many of them also had piercings in various parts of their
5 bodies. Some people admire body art, but others don't understand why
anyone wants these "ugly" things on their beautiful bodies. Doctors are
concerned about the health risks of tattooing and piercing.

Possible Health Problems

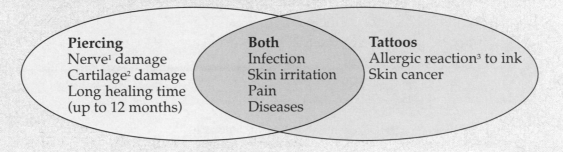

Piercing
Nerve[1] damage
Cartilage[2] damage
Long healing time
(up to 12 months)

Both
Infection
Skin irritation
Pain
Diseases

Tattoos
Allergic reaction[3] to ink
Skin cancer

---

[1] **nerve:** a fiber that connects the body organs to the brain or spinal cord
[2] **cartilage:** strong elastic tissue in the outer ear and around bones
[3] **allergic reaction:** a physical response, such as sneezing or a skin rash

There is a high risk of getting blood-transmitted diseases, such as Hepatitis B and AIDS because many tattoo and piercing parlors don't take basic disease-preventing precautions like using new latex gloves, new needles, and new pots of ink for each client. Doctors strongly suggest that people take the following precautions before they get tattooed or pierced:

- Get a vaccination[4] for Hepatitis B.

- Set limits (wear one or two earrings, not five).

- Find a reliable parlor or doctor who uses sterile[5] needles.

- Keep tattooed and pierced areas clean.

When someone considers getting a piercing or tattoo, safety and health are key concerns, but there is another issue as well. While teens and young adults may be happy with their tattoos at first, as they age they often change their minds. In addition, when relationships fall apart, people no longer want to have an ex-boyfriend's or ex-girlfriend's name on their bodies. In fact, some people keep their tattoos covered up with long sleeves. These changes of heart keep dermatologist Lynn Grossfeld busy. Dr. Grossfeld has removed over 6,000 tattoos from people who regret getting them. It's not an easy process: most tattoos are painful and expensive to remove. If you feel you must get a tattoo, Grossfeld suggests, "Choose a small one and put it in place that doesn't show."

While some people may not appreciate the "art" in body art, Americans are learning to accept it as a form of self-expression. However, along with greater acceptance, there has been an increase in body art and more health problems. Understanding the risks and trying to prevent the problems is the smart way to enjoy body art.

---

[4] **vaccination:** an injection, or shot, that prevents a disease
[5] **sterile:** very clean, free from germs and dirt

14 SHARE WHAT YOU LEARNED

A. Work with a partner who read the same article.

   1. Read the focus questions for your article in the chart below.

   2. Discuss the questions and write the answers.

FOCUS QUESTIONS FOR TEXT A

1. How many people in the study had tattoos and piercings?

2. Give four reasons why people get body art.

3. Besides body art, what are some other ways people change their appearance?

4. Throughout history, why have people tried to change their physical appearance?

FOCUS QUESTIONS FOR TEXT B

1. How many people in the study had tattoos and piercings?

1. What are some health problems that body art can cause?

2. What can someone do to prevent the health problems?

3. What are some reasons people remove their tattoos or piercings?

B. With your partner, find a pair who read a different text and form a team.

   1. Share the topic of your text with your teammates.

   2. Take turns sharing the answers to the focus questions.

   3. Add any other information from the text that you remember.

15 SHARE WHAT YOU THINK

Discuss these questions with your teammates. Then share your answers with the class.

1. In your opinion, does the attraction of body art outweigh the health risks?

2. Do you think body art is simply an act of rebellion by young people, or is it an important part of American culture? Explain.

3. Do you think the young people of today will choose to keep their body art or remove it when they get older? Why?

4. What are some other cultures where body art is popular? What type of body art do people in those cultures have?

16 REFLECT ON WHAT YOU READ IN THIS UNIT

Survey and Chart

A. Answer the questions below. Then survey nine classmates. Use tick marks (卌) to record all the responses.

Question	Yes	No
1. Should businesses have casual dress days?		
2. Should there be a minimum age for body art?		

B. Look at the bar graph below. Then make a similar graph to show how many students answered "yes" to each question in the survey. Discuss the results of your survey with your classmates. Use expressions such as:

Nine out of ten people . . .   *A majority of people . . .*   *Only a few people . . .*

# of students	Support casual dress in business	Support a minimum age for body art
10		
9		
8		
7		
6		
5		
4		
3		
2		
1		

Interview and Write

A. Interview a partner. Ask these questions about appearance and take notes on your partner's answers.

1. What's the first thing you notice when you meet someone new? Why?

2. Does the way someone looks affect the way you feel about them? Why or why not? Give examples.

3. Is your appearance (clothing, hair length, body art, etc.) similar to that of your friends? Why or why not? Does this affect your friendship? Why or why not?

B. Use your notes to write one or more paragraphs about your partner's ideas.

Research

Read more about the topic of appearance.

1. Use the Internet or an encyclopedia to look up *body art*, *casual dress*, *body image*, or *tattoo*.

2. Read and take notes on one or more sections of the article you choose.

3. Bring your notes to class and report on the information you found.

Unit 4

Getting the News

In this unit you will:

- read about sources of news in the U.S.
- learn how to understand vocabulary in context

HOW DO YOU LEARN ABOUT EVENTS IN THE NEWS?

A. Look at the picture. How is this woman getting the news? Why? Discuss your ideas with your classmates.

B. Think about these questions. Discuss your answers with a partner. Then share your ideas with your classmates.

1. Do you prefer to get news from a newspaper, TV, radio, or the Internet? Why?

2. Do you believe what you read or hear in the news? Do you think most news reports are true? Why or why not?

3. Which of the following news topics interests you most: politics, sports, business, or entertainment? Why?

A. Answer the questions in the chart below. Then survey nine other students. Use tick marks (卌) to record all the responses.

HOW MUCH TIME EACH DAY DO YOU SPEND DOING THE FOLLOWING ACTIVITIES?				
Activity	0–30 min.	30 min.–2hrs.	2–4 hrs.	4+ hrs.
1. watching TV news shows				
2. listening to radio news shows				
3. reading newspapers				
4. reading magazines				
5. using the Internet to get news				

B. Discuss the results of the survey with your classmates. Use the following expressions:

Nine out of ten people…   *The majority of the people…*   *Only a few people…*

C. Read the sentences below. Guess which phrase has a meaning similar to the underlined word or phrase, and highlight it. Check your guesses after you read the article on pages 52–53.

1. For truthful information, the public depends on journalists, the people who gather, write, and report the news.

2. TV and radio stations let the public know all the important things that happen in their community. They report these events on their news programs.

3. Technology can also deliver news. Some people get their news on the Internet, or through their computers or cell phones.

4. Some cable TV stations offer continuous news reports. They give information 24 hours a day.

5. A news source may be a magazine, newspaper, radio or TV show, or the Internet. Each offers information about local, national, and world news.

6. Internet companies compete with newspapers and magazines. They try to do better by updating their reports more often, usually several times a day.

7. The Internet attracts many people. It gets the attention of those who like to use computers.

8. Thanks to the media, the public can stay up-to-date on the news. Newspapers, radio, TV, and the Internet all provide a great deal of information.

> **Using context clues** means getting information about the meaning of key words in a text by looking at the words or phrases nearby. You can usually find these clues in the same sentence or paragraph as the key word. Clues can be definitions, examples, synonyms (words with a similar meaning), or contrasting words or phrases. Sometimes part of the clue is a signal—a particular word or phrase that can help you identify the clue.

Type of Clue	Some Signals	Sample Sentence
Definition	*means, or*	The lives of journalists, or people who write the news, are often exciting.
Example	*for example, including, such as*	Computer-based technology, such as the Internet, can deliver the news very quickly.
Synonym	*in other words, or, sometimes called, that is*	The public can now get continuous, or ongoing, reporting of the news.
Contrast	*but, however, instead of, not, unlike*	Unlike other news sources, TV holds our attention with powerful pictures.

Practice Using Context Clues

Read the paragraph below. Circle each signal you find. Then highlight the words and phrases that tell you the meaning of the underlined words. Label each type of clue. Compare answers with a partner.

Sources of Information

For hundreds of years, people learned about the world from materials in print, such as books, newspapers, and magazines. This was the main way people acquired, or got, information. Literacy, or the ability to read and write, was the key to learning. Today many people also get their information from electronic media. They prefer to watch television, listen to the radio or connect to the Internet rather than reading. That's why it's important for students to learn to analyze, not just accept, electronic information as well as what they read in print.

example
_____
_____

_____

_____

Use Your Reading Skills

A. Preview the article below and the comprehension questions on page 54, exercise A. Then discuss these questions with your classmates.

1. What is the topic of the article?

2. What do you already know about the topic?

3. What do you predict you will learn from the article?

B. As you read the article, highlight the clues that help you understand these words. They are underlined in the article.

a. assassination	b. technology	c. on demand
d. request	e. objectively	f. sensationalism

3 READ

This magazine article discusses how technology has changed the way people get the news in the United States. In the 21st century, people don't have to wait for a newspaper delivery or a TV news program. By using technology, they can get the news any time of day or night.

High-Tech News

Traditional Sources of News

In 1963 Americans watched Walter Cronkite, the most popular TV journalist of the time, report the
5 assassination of John F. Kennedy. People stayed in front of their TVs for days after the killing of their president. They read the morning newspapers and turned on car
10 radios in order to follow every single piece of news about this national tragedy.[1] For the next 30 years or so, most people got their news the same way—they watched
15 television, listened to the radio, or read the newspaper. For every important news event, such as the landing of men on the moon, the nation turned to these news
20 sources to find out what was happening.

News Technology

In the 21st century, advances in technology such as the Internet,
25 satellite[2] and cable TV, and cellular phones now allow the public to get news 24 hours a day on demand, or whenever they want it. Cable TV stations such as CNN™ provide "all
30 news all the time"—continuous reporting of news as it happens. The Internet offers summaries of the news almost every time people

[1] **tragedy:** an event that causes extreme sadness
[2] **satellite:** a spacecraft that is sent into orbit around the earth in order to send television and telephone signals to earth

go on-line. There are also many websites that make it easy to follow news events from beginning to end. All you have to do is type in the topic that interests you, and the story you want comes on the screen, along with links[3] to related stories. Some people connect to radio station websites via the Internet, where they can listen to 24-hour news radio or hear discussions about the news on talk radio.

Thanks to the Internet, it's possible for people to get their own personal news reports on specific topics. A doctor might request information about a certain new medicine. A farmer might ask about new techniques for growing corn. In response, an information service gathers the latest news on each topic, analyzes it, creates a special report, and e-mails the requested information to the customer.

Competition for Customers

High-tech sources of news, especially the Internet, are trying to attract people who usually read newspapers or watch TV, and they are succeeding. More than half of the population, or 150 million Americans, used the Internet in 2003, many of them getting some news on-line. Nicholas Negroponte of the Massachusetts Institute of Technology predicts that Americans will soon spend more time on the Internet than watching television.

In order to compete with the Internet, some newspapers and TV stations are changing the way they deliver the news. Instead of reporting the news objectively, basing their stories on facts, they try to keep their readers' and viewers' interest by focusing on the most upsetting or shocking details of a story. This trend toward sensationalism is making people question the truth of the news. According to one study, 55% of Americans used to believe what they heard or read in news reports. Recently, that number has dropped to 29% for television and even lower for newspapers and magazines.

The Winner

As in every business, competing for customers is a key concern for news media companies. Today people in the United States have a wide variety of news sources to choose from. While some people prefer computer-based sources, most still get their news from traditional sources. It will be interesting to see which type of source—high tech or traditional— wins the competition in the future.

Adapted from *The World & I Magazine*

[3] **link:** an address on a website that refers to another site on a similar topic

A. Answer the questions. Then discuss your answers with a partner. Look back at the article on pages 52–53 to check your answers.

1. How did Americans get their news in the 1960s?

2. What are two ways people use technology to get news today? Describe them.

3. Why do traditional and high-tech news sources compete with each other? What have some traditional news sources done in order to compete?

4. According to the article, how do most people get their news?

B. Choose the idea under each heading that does not appear in the article. Look back at the article on pages 52–53 to check your answers.

1. Traditional Sources of News

    a. In the 20th century, most people got their news from computers.
    b. In 1963, Americans got their news from three main sources.
    c. People want to know all about important news events.

2. News Technology

    a. In the 21st century, people can get news any time.
    b. People can get news reports on topics they want to learn about.
    c. Personal news reports are not available now.

3. Competition for Customers

    a. Some journalists are not basing their stories on facts.
    b. Americans' belief in the truth of news reports has not changed.
    c. A majority of Americans use the Internet.

4. The Winner

    a. Americans use all kinds of media to get the news.
    b. Most Americans get their news from high-tech sources.
    c. Many Americans listen to the radio to get the news.

C. Think about these questions. Then discuss them with your classmates.

1. Which type of news source do you think will win the competition for customers in the future? Why? Use information from the article to support your opinion.

2. How do you think traditional news sources can regain the trust of the people?

3. Imagine you can get a personal news report. Which news topic will you request? Why?

5 WORK WITH THE VOCABULARY

A. Match the words with their definitions.

___ 1. journalist   a. TV, radio, newspapers, and the Internet used as a means of communication

___ 2. media   b. a newspaper, TV show, etc.

___ 3. continuous   c. try to do better than someone else

___ 4. technology   d. electronic or digital products or systems

___ 5. news source   e. get attention or interest

___ 6. compete   f. something important that happens

___ 7. attract   g. a person who gathers, writes, and reports the news

___ 8. event   h. ongoing, without stopping

B. Fill in the missing adjectives and nouns in the chart. Look back at the article on pages 52–53 to find the correct forms.

Adjective	Noun	Paragraph
	popularity	1
	nation	1
informational		3
technological		2
	tradition	6
competitive		6

C. Choose the correct form of the word for each sentence. Write a sentence with the word you didn't choose.

1. Watching TV news was an American ((tradition)/traditional) for 30 years.
   Traditional news sources include radio, newspapers, and TV.

2. Both TV and radio have (information/informational) programs.

3. (Competition/competitive) is very strong among different news sources.

4. The (popularity/popular) of high-tech news sources is growing.

5. People can get local, state, or (nation/national) news on the Internet.

6. There will be many (technology/technological) advances in media in the future.

A. Write the answers to these questions. Then discuss your answers with your classmates.

1. What do you think are the elements of a successful TV news program?

2. How do TV programs hold the interest of viewers?

3. How do you think the TV networks decide which programs to keep showing?

4. What type of news programs do you like to watch? Why?

B. Read the sentences below. Guess which word or phrase has a meaning similar to the underlined word. Highlight your guesses and check them after you read the article on pages 57–58.

1. Sometimes the news is very <u>dramatic</u>. It has the same powerful, exciting qualities as a good play.

2. Journalists like to report about <u>heroes</u>. Brave people who do courageous things are often the focus of news stories.

3. Some news stories are very enjoyable and hold viewers' interest. These types of stories often <u>entertain</u> the people who watch them.

4. Certain types of TV shows <u>appeal</u> to teenagers. The programs that feature music, humor, or movie stars are very interesting to young people.

5. Many adults like shows about <u>political</u> events. They think it's important to know about government issues.

6. Popular programs usually have high <u>ratings</u>. The networks keep track of how many people watch these programs every week.

7. Some people have a negative <u>attitude</u> toward TV news. Their feeling is that the programs they watch don't always show the truth.

8. When journalists go out looking for news stories, they often have exciting and dangerous experiences. Then they report on their <u>adventures</u>.

Use Your Reading Skills

A. Preview the article on pages 57–58. Then answer these questions.

1. What is the topic of this article?

2. What do you already know about the topic?

3. What do you predict you will learn from this article?

B. Read the article quickly, skipping any words you don't know. Time your reading. Write the start time at the top and the end time at the bottom. Then answer the questions on page 58, section 8, exercise A.

🕐 **Start time** _____

The television networks have created a different type of news program called a Mediathon. This newspaper article asks the following question: Is the Mediathon a serious look at important events, or is it just another form of entertainment?

The Mediathon—An Interesting Way to Get the News

When it comes to the news, Americans seem to be saying, "Don't just tell us the news, tell us a story." This attitude has made one
5 kind of television program very popular: the Mediathon. Like the sagas of the past, Mediathons often tell stories of exciting adventures, brave heroes, or terrible tragedies.
10 To create a Mediathon, TV news journalists choose an important news event and entertain viewers by reporting on it 24 hours-a-day for days and sometimes weeks. The
15 networks try to make the news program more entertaining by playing special music or by using a logo, or symbol for the show. Mediathons appeal to many people
20 and make a lot of money for the TV networks. This huge profit is one of the main reasons why these programs have become very common.

A famous example of an American
25 political Mediathon was *Election 2000*. This was the story of the presidential race between Vice President Al Gore and Governor George W. Bush. Problems in the
30 voting process caused a long delay in the final count of the vote. No one knew the result of the election for several weeks. During this time, there was round-the-clock coverage,
35 or news reporting, of the court battles that finally led to a decision. Every day the TV audience heard discussions of the situation by journalists as well as experts who
40 knew a lot about politics and law. The news programs repeated the same story again and again until there was some new information to add. As the story developed, viewers
45 watched history become a dramatic TV miniseries.

Shows such as *Election 2000* continue to be popular. They appeal to people's curiosity, their desire to
50 know all about something. Even more important, the shows are exciting and they hold the attention of the audience. William Randolph Hearst, a well-known American
55 publisher, said, "the public is even more fond of entertainment than it is of information." Hearst understood that knowing what the audience likes is a key to the success of the media.
60 The Mediathon is successful, but it is also controversial.[1] Many people believe that the role of journalism in American society is to protect democracy[2] by simply reporting the
65 facts. For them, the Mediathon is just entertainment, a "media circus," and not true journalism. Other people believe that the Mediathon has a

---

[1] **controversial:** causing public discussion and disagreement
[2] **democracy:** a system in which people elect representatives to run the government

positive effect on society because it encourages people to watch the news and keep up with current events.

Good or bad, the Mediathon will be around until declining TV ratings show that people are no longer interested. So far the ratings aren't dropping at all. In fact, Mediathons are so popular that even when there is no important news event, the networks often show an update of an old story.

Since ancient times, sagas have satisfied people's need for stories. Now in the 21st century, the Mediathon is meeting that need. Instead of reading tales of heroes, sacrifice,[3] and tragedy, people in the United States now look to the news media to tell them a good story.

Adapted from the *New York Times*

[3] **sacrifice:** an act of giving something up in order to help others

 **End time** _____

8 PROCESS WHAT YOU READ

A. Mark the statements true (T) or false (F) without looking back at the article. Check your answers on page 131. Follow the instructions for recording your comprehension score and reading speed on the inside back cover.

____ **1.** A Mediathon is a weekly 30-minute TV program.

____ **2.** TV networks produce Mediathons because they make money.

____ **3.** All Mediathons have a logo and special music.

____ **4.** Some people dislike Mediathons because they simply report the facts.

____ **5.** Others like Mediathons because they get people to watch the news.

B. What do you like about Mediathons? What do you dislike about them? Discuss your answers with your classmates.

9 WORK WITH THE VOCABULARY

A. Scan the article on pages 57–58 to find these words. Highlight the context clues for each one.

a. sagas	b. logo	c. profit	d. experts
e. curiosity	f. fond of	g. media circus	h. declining

B. Write a question using each of the words below. Then ask a partner your questions.

a. adventure	b. appeal	c. attitude	d. dramatic	e. hero	f. political

What type of news programs appeal to you?

A. **Look at the cartoon and answer the questions below. Discuss your ideas with your classmates.**

"Dennis, I would like to talk to you for a minute—off-line."

1. What is this cartoon saying about technology and communication?

2. Do you communicate more in person, on-line, or by telephone? Why?

B. **Put a check (✓) next to the words you know. Ask your classmates for the meanings of the words you don't know. Look up the words no one knows in a dictionary.**

____ anonymous   ____ companionship

____ connection   ____ humorous

____ leisure   ____ precaution

____ relate to   ____ social life

C. **Preview the two texts on pages 60–62. Then answer these questions.**

1. What is the topic of text A?

2. What is the topic of text B?

D. **Choose one text to read. Then answer these questions.**

1. What is the title of your text?

2. What do you already know about this topic?

3. What do you think you will learn about the topic?

E. **As you read the article, find at least three words that are defined in context and highlight the context clues. Compare answers with your classmates.**

In the United States, listening to the radio is one of the main ways people get information. This magazine article discusses "talk radio," which allows people not only to gather but also to share information.

Talk Radio Explosion

Americans spend a great deal of time listening to the radio. Many of the most popular programs are "talk shows,"
5 which feature[1] conversation rather than music. Approximately 52 million people listen to talk radio and many of them share their thoughts by telephone, fax,
10 or e-mail.

Some listeners choose serious radio programs that discuss the news or social, economic, and political issues. On other stations,
15 experts talk about a wide range of topics, such as psychology, history, or science. Many people enjoy talk shows that give advice in humorous or entertaining
20 ways. These popular programs offer information about car repair, travel, restaurants, health, pet care, gardening, and finance. Listeners to all these shows can
25 call or write in to ask questions or respond.

Talk radio wasn't always so popular in the United States. In 1980 there were only 75
30 talk-only radio stations. Today there are more than 1,350. Sylvia Rimm, psychologist and former host of the talk radio show *Family Talk*, thinks there
35 are good reasons why Americans listen to talk radio; the most important one is listener participation. Talk shows are successful because they are
40 interactive—they encourage listeners to take part in the discussion. Rimm says that Americans seem to have a great need to talk to each other. For
45 example, women who work outside the home don't have the social life they could have if they stayed home and saw friends and neighbors during the day.
50 Now they turn to talk radio to listen to other people and share their ideas.

The fact that callers can stay anonymous is another reason
55 why talk shows are so successful. People don't have to say who they are or use their correct names. Sometimes callers have questions or problems that
60 they're too embarrassed to discuss with friends or family.

[1] **feature:** to have as an important element

On talk radio, these people can get answers to their questions or help with their problems without 65 giving any personal information.

Cell phones, laptop computers, satellite technology, and the Internet make it possible for even more people to access, or 70 tune in to, talk radio. "Out of the 2,000 radio stations that are 'Webcasting' (broadcasting on the Internet), one in five is a talk station," says Michael Packer, 75 president of Packer Talk Radio Consulting. "That means a lot of people are now listening to talk radio through the Internet." Now wherever people are, 80 anywhere in the world, they can listen and respond by phone, e-mail, or fax.

Talk radio satisfies a need for information as well as for contact 85 and companionship. "In our high-tech society," says Packer, "talk radio makes 'high tech' also 'high touch.' It provides a connection to other people. We 90 hear other people's opinions and say, 'I can relate to that.'"

Adapted from *The World & I Magazine*

12 READ B

More than 150 million people in the United States use the Internet to learn about the world around them. This website discusses a personal approach to getting information: on-line chatting.

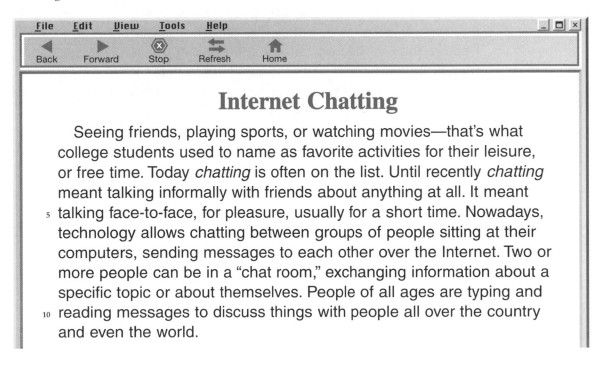

File   Edit   View   Tools   Help

Back   Forward   Stop   Refresh   Home

Internet Chatting

Seeing friends, playing sports, or watching movies—that's what college students used to name as favorite activities for their leisure, or free time. Today *chatting* is often on the list. Until recently *chatting* meant talking informally with friends about anything at all. It meant 5 talking face-to-face, for pleasure, usually for a short time. Nowadays, technology allows chatting between groups of people sitting at their computers, sending messages to each other over the Internet. Two or more people can be in a "chat room," exchanging information about a specific topic or about themselves. People of all ages are typing and 10 reading messages to discuss things with people all over the country and even the world.

Internet chatting is popular because it's an easy way to have a social life. More than 25 percent of people in the United States who go on-line use chat rooms. That's 37 million people! People can talk
15 about a variety of topics on chat sites—from sports, to art and music, to business, science, and health. Katie, a college student from Minnesota, chats about college life a couple of times a week with a group of 20–25 other chatters. She says, "People are so quick to judge you when you meet them in person. I don't want to worry about
20 what people think of my hair or my clothes. I just want to talk."

With Internet chat, making friends has become much easier. Typing on a computer takes away the shy or awkward[1] feelings that often go along with meeting new people in person. On-line, people often feel freer to talk.

25 Some people start out looking for information about topics that interest them and end up finding companionship or even love. On-line chatters sometimes learn so much about each other, that they develop strong relationships. Other Internet users subscribe to websites that pair compatible[2] people. One dating website has over
30 2.1 million registered users. They say that there have been more than 650 marriages as a result of chatting on their site.

Using chat rooms can be interesting and fun, but sharing information with strangers requires that chatters take precautions. One website publishes safety tips for people meeting on-line and off. The site
35 advises chatters to stay anonymous by not giving their real names or information about where they live and work. When chatters meet in person, they should be careful to meet in a public place and bring friends along. Following these basic rules helps keep people safe.

Psychologists today often note that Americans have a great need
40 to connect with others, and in the fast-paced modern world this is not always easy. Chat rooms provide new opportunities for connection. They create communities of people with shared interests, and sometimes, with long-lasting results. In a chat room, a simple exchange of information may turn into a satisfying, life-long friendship.

[1] **awkward:** embarrassed, not relaxed
[2] **compatible:** able to go together well; well-matched

13 SHARE WHAT YOU LEARNED

A. Work with a partner who read the same article.

1. Read the focus questions for your article in the chart below.

2. Discuss the questions and write the answers.

FOCUS QUESTIONS FOR TEXT A
1. What is talk radio and how many people in the U.S. listen to it?
2. Why is talk radio popular?
3. What emotional needs does talk radio satisfy?
4. How has technology helped the growth of talk radio?

FOCUS QUESTIONS FOR TEXT B
1. What is "chatting" and how many people in the U.S. chat on-line?
2. Why is Internet chatting popular?
3. What emotional needs does chatting satisfy?
4. What are some precautions Internet chatters should take?

B. With your partner, find a pair who read a different text and form a team.

1. Share the topic of your text with your teammates.

2. Take turns sharing the answers to the focus questions.

3. Add any other information from the text that you remember.

14 SHARE WHAT YOU THINK

Discuss these questions with your teammates. Then share your answers with the class.

1. How are talk radio and Internet chatting similar? How are they different?

2. What is your opinion of talk radio? Do you think it's popular in countries other than the U.S.? Why or why not?

3. What subjects do you think are most popular in Internet chatting? Do you think there's a difference in the way men and women chat over the Internet? Explain.

4. Have you or your friends ever listened to talk radio or chatted on-line? Tell about your experiences.

15 REFLECT ON WHAT YOU READ IN THIS UNIT

Interview

Think about your answers to these questions. Interview your partner. Then decide together which news source is most effective.

1. How is TV news different from the news you get on the radio, in the newspaper, or on the Internet? How do these differences affect the information?

2. Do you trust some new sources more than others? Why or why not?

Chart and Write

A. Work in small groups. Think of positive, negative, and interesting aspects of TV news. Look at the statements in the chart. Write one more idea in each section of the chart.

WHAT DO YOU THINK ABOUT TV NEWS?		
Positive	**Negative**	**Interesting**
People keep up on current events.	Sometimes the news isn't reported objectively.	Some news programs are similar to sagas.

B. Use the information in the chart to write a paragraph that contrasts the positive and negative aspects of TV news. Use the ideas in the "Interesting" column also.

16 REFLECT ON YOUR READING STRATEGIES

A. Read the questions in the chart and choose the answers that best describe your use of the reading strategies. Then with your classmates, discuss which strategies are the most helpful.

Strategy	How often do you use this strategy outside of this class?			How helpful is this strategy?		
	Always	**Sometimes**	**Never**	**Very**	**A little**	**Not**
Previewing and Predicting						
Scanning						
Skipping words						
Using context clues						

B. Tell a partner which strategies are easiest for you and which strategies you need to practice more.

Unit 5

Feeding Body and Soul

In this unit you will:

- read about mealtime in the U.S.
- learn how to find the main idea and supporting details

HOW IMPORTANT IS MEALTIME IN THE U.S.?

A. Look at the picture. Do you think it represents a typical mealtime for a family in the U.S.? Why or why not? Does it represent a typical mealtime for your family or friends? Why or why not? Discuss your ideas with your classmates.

B. Think about these statements. Do you agree or disagree? Discuss your answers with a partner. Then share your ideas with your classmates.

1. It's important for a family to eat meals together.

2. Food satisfies the emotions as well as the body.

3. Fast food and home-cooked food both make good meals.

A. Answer the questions in the chart. Then survey nine classmates. Record all the responses with tick marks (ⱽ⧧⧧).

How often do you . . .	Every day	4–6 times a week	2–3 times a week	Once a week	Never
1. cook dinner?					
2. share a meal with family?					
3. share a meal with friends?					
4. eat in a restaurant?					
5. eat fast food?					
6. eat alone?					
7. eat in front of the TV?					
8. eat in the car?					

B. Discuss the results of your survey with your classmates. Use expressions such as:

The majority of students . . .   *Nine out of ten students . . .*   *Only a few people . . .*

C. Read the sentences below. Guess which word or phrase has a meaning similar to the underlined words. Highlight your guesses, and check them as you read the article on pages 68–69.

1. Good food improves our <u>physical</u> health. It gives our bodies the vitamins and minerals it needs.

2. Just as we feed our bodies with food, we <u>nourish</u> our minds with good books.

3. A cup of soup is <u>comforting</u> after a hard day at work. Having something warm and delicious often makes you feel better.

4. When you <u>savor</u> a dish, you eat it slowly in order to taste all the flavors and really enjoy it.

5. Your nose first identifies a great meal by its <u>scent</u>. The pleasant smells of the food help you taste it more fully.

6. On holidays, people often have a big meal. A holiday <u>feast</u> is usually made up of many home-cooked dishes.

7. People have a <u>snack</u> when they get hungry between meals. They usually eat a small amount of food at that time in order to save room for lunch or dinner.

8. Food and good company can help you relax and forget your worries. For example, it's good to eat a nice dinner after the <u>stress</u> of a difficult day.

2 BUILDING READING SKILLS: Finding the Main Idea and Supporting Details

The **main ideas** in a text are the ideas or points that the author thinks are the most important. There is usually a main idea in each paragraph of a text. Often you will find it in the first sentence. Other sentences in the paragraph provide **supporting details** that give specific information about the main idea. To identify the main idea in a paragraph, ask yourself, "What point does the author want to make about the topic?"

Practice Finding the Main Idea and Supporting Details

A. The phrases in each item are from one paragraph. Label the phrase that is the main idea with *m* and the phrases that are supporting details with *d*.

1. _d_ a. Thanksgiving dinner
    _m_ b. holiday meals
    _d_ c. Fourth of July picnic

2. ___ a. family dinners
    ___ b. cook together
    ___ c. discuss the day's events

3. ___ a. chop vegetables
    ___ b. roast meat
    ___ c. make dinner

4. ___ a. dessert
    ___ b. lunch
    ___ c. soup

B. Read the text below. Then answer the questions. Compare answers with a partner.

> ### *Family Meals in the United States*
>
> In many American homes, family members spend approximately 38 minutes preparing dinner, but the average family spends only 26 minutes eating together. What's even more surprising is that 27 percent of families spend less than 20 minutes at the dinner table. Many families often spend more time preparing dinner than eating it.
>
> Despite these statistics, there are still several popular mealtime customs that bring a family together. One thing many families do regularly is assign each person a task, such as setting the table or making a dish. Another important custom is sharing stories about the day's events. In addition, some families have a special afternoon or evening meal together on weekends.

1. What is the topic of the text?
2. What is the main idea of the first paragraph? In which sentence did you find it?
3. What is one supporting detail in the first paragraph?
4. What is the main idea of the second paragraph? In which sentence did you find it?
5. What is one supporting detail in the second paragraph?

Use Your Reading Skills

Preview the article below. Then read the first paragraph. Work with a partner to answer these questions.

1. What is the topic of the article?

2. What is the main idea of the first paragraph?

3. In which sentence did you find the main idea?

4. What is one supporting detail?

3 READ

When television and fast food became popular, the American custom of eating together was almost lost. This magazine article discusses the rediscovery of the benefits of sharing meals.

FEEDING THE SOUL

Many Americans remember the sweet scent of apple pie baking in their ovens, or the warmth of homemade
5 macaroni and cheese cooking on the stove. The memories of these comforting foods include not only the dishes themselves, but also the people who
10 prepared them and ate them together. "Cooking and eating those delicious foods at home was the way we strengthened relationships, the way we
15 showed we cared for each other," says cookbook writer Marion Cunningham. Food was more than calories[1] and nutrients[2] for the body; it
20 was nourishment for the soul as well.

The last half of the 20th century marked a big change in American eating habits. Up
25 until the 1950s, people cooked and ate most meals at home. Then television arrived, and so did the TV dinner—a frozen meal on a metal tray
30 that people could heat in the oven and eat while they watched TV. The TV dinner was one of the many time-savers that helped women get out of
35 the kitchen and into the job market. Once people left the table to eat in front of the TV, it wasn't so different for them to eat fast food alone in their
40 cars. By the 1990s, the average American was eating several meals in the car each week, and the joy of eating at home with family was almost forgotten.
45 Nowadays, many Americans are starting to realize what

[1] **calorie:** a unit of energy in food. Calories affect a person's weight.
[2] **nutrient:** a substance in foods, such as a mineral or vitamin, that helps living things grow

they have lost, and they're returning to meals that nourish both the body and the
50 soul. More often, they are sitting down with friends and family to savor nature's gifts: the large variety of ethnic foods, the farm-grown fruits
55 and vegetables, and the home-cooked meals that help us remember the flavors of childhood. Food for the soul can range from a multicourse
60 feast with one's family over a long Sunday afternoon, to a late-night snack with a friend.

Scientists agree that food affects the spirit as well
65 as the body. According to pharmacologist Candace Pert of Georgetown University, the digestive system[3] doesn't only process food; it's also a major
70 emotional center. Pert says, "Food acts as a natural tranquilizer[4] by causing the release of hormones[5] that reduce stress." In this way,
75 eating sends messages of well-being to the brain.

The feelings of pleasure that result from sharing meals can also improve physical health.
80 Medical research shows that people who feel connected to a supportive network of family and friends often have longer, healthier lives. Dr. Herbert
85 Benson, associate professor at Harvard Medical School, firmly believes that delicious food and pleasant company make eating a healthy and soulful
90 experience. Benson, one of the authors of *The Wellness Book*, advises people to relax during meals and to focus on the tastes and textures[6] of the
95 food. Friendly conversation is also important, since feeding the soul requires good feelings as well as good tastes.

So how do we know if we're
100 eating soulfully? There is no one answer, but Thomas Moore, author of the best-selling book *Care of the Soul* offers two hints: "Shop for
105 local, fresh food. Eat with variety." According to Moore, cooking at home also nourishes the body and the soul. He writes, "Preparing
110 food is like magic.[7] You see transformations right in front of you. You pour batter in a pan, and heat it for so long, and you've got a cake—a whole
115 different thing. Our souls need such magic."

Adapted from the *Minneapolis Star Tribune*

[3] **digestive system:** the organs (stomach, intestines, etc.) that change food so the body can use it
[4] **tranquilizer:** something that has a calming effect on people. It's often a drug, but not always
[5] **hormone:** a chemical in the body that affects the body's growth and condition
[6] **texture:** the way something feels when you touch it or eat it, e.g., soft
[7] **magic:** a power that makes impossible things happen

4 PROCESS WHAT YOU READ

A. Answer the questions. Then discuss your answers with a partner. Look back at the article on pages 68–69 to check your answers.

1. How did Americans eat before the 1950s? What caused eating habits to change?

2. How are Americans changing their eating habits in the 21st century? Why?

3. According to some doctors and scientists, what are the emotional benefits of food? What are the physical benefits of eating with other people?

4. What are three ways to feed the soul?

B. Look back at paragraphs 2, 3, 4, and 5 in the article. For each paragraph, choose the sentence below that best states the main idea.

Paragraph 2

    a. In the 1950s, Americans cooked and ate at home.
    b. Starting in the 1950s, Americans began to eat differently.
    c. In the 1950s, TV dinners saved time.

Paragraph 3

    a. Nowadays, Americans feed their souls with a feast or a snack.
    b. Nowadays, Americans eat home-cooked meals.
    c. Nowadays, Americans want food to feed the body and the soul.

Paragraph 4

    a. Eating helps people feel good.
    b. Scientists believe that food is good for the body and the soul.
    c. The digestive system is a center for the emotions.

Paragraph 5

    a. Eating with others makes people healthier.
    b. Staying relaxed during a meal is healthy.
    c. Tasty food makes dining a healthy experience.

C. Think about these questions. Then discuss them with your classmates.

1. The article says "Preparing food is like magic." Do you agree or disagree? Why?

2. What are some comforting foods you remember from your childhood?

3. Do you eat "soulfully"? Explain.

5 WORK WITH THE VOCABULARY

A. Scan the article on pages 68–69 to see how the author uses each of the following words in context. Then work with a partner to write new sentences using the words. Share your sentences with your classmates.

a. scent	b. comforting	c. nourish	d. savor
e. feast	f. snack	g. stress	h. physical

B. Fill in the missing adjectives and nouns in the chart. Look back at the article to find the correct forms.

Adjective	Noun	Paragraph
soulful		1
memorable		1
	emotion	4
pleasurable		5
	support	5
	health	5

C. Choose the correct form of the word for each sentence.

1. Eating with family and friends is good for your (health /healthy).

2. Sharing meals with others is also good for the (soul/soulful).

3. Food affects not only the body but also the (emotions/emotional).

4. It can be (pleasure/pleasurable) to share food with family and friends.

5. It feels good to have a (support/supportive) group of friends.

6. Eating with others can be a (memory/memorable) event.

D. Words sometimes have more than one meaning. Look at the following words and the phrases that define them. Choose the meanings that are used in the article. Look back at the article to check your answers.

1. tastes: a. flavor
              b. personal preferences, the types of things one likes

2. network: a. a group of radio or television broadcasting stations
              b. a large group of people who help each other

3. company: a. companionship
              b. a business

6 GET READY TO READ ABOUT: A Memorable Meal

A. Look at the web diagram below. Make a similar diagram about a special meal that you remember. Replace the questions in the circles with your answers. Discuss your answers with a partner. Keep the web you make. You will use it later.

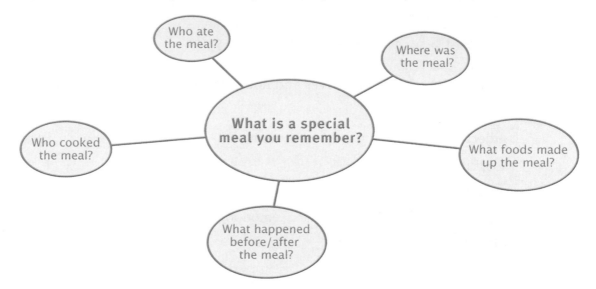

B. Put a check (✓) next to the words you know. Ask your classmates for the meanings of the words you don't know. Look up the words no one knows in a dictionary.

____ combination   ____ cupboard   ____ elder   ____ endless

____ ingredient   ____ leftovers   ____ portion   ____ prove

Use Your Reading Skills

A. Preview the article on pages 73–74. Read the first paragraph and the last paragraph. Work with a partner to answer these questions about each paragraph you read.

1. What is the topic of the paragraph?

2. What is the main idea?

3. In which sentence did you find the main idea?

4. What is one detail that supports the main idea?

B. Read the article quickly, skipping any words you don't know. Time yourself. Put the start time at the top and the end time at the bottom. Then answer the questions on page 74, section 8.

Antonio Sacre makes his living as a storyteller. In his stories, he often talks about growing up in Miami's Cuban American community. In this story he describes Cuban food and the person who taught him to love it.

My Last Meal
A N T O N I O   S A C R E

When I think of my last meal on earth, it's not just the actual dishes themselves that I desire; it's the memory of eating them with the person who made them in her house—my *abuela*, my grandmother Mimi. The meal itself
5 is simple: rice, beans, some type of meat, fried green and ripe plantains, avocado, and onions drizzled in oil. My grandmother could take these few ingredients and create a seemingly endless combination of dishes: white rice or yellow rice; red, black, brown, green, or white beans; chicken, beef, pork, fish, or *chorizo* (sausage)—fried, baked, roasted, or stewed. There were many different types of salads,
10 and Cuban bread fresh from the *panadería*. There was also a dazzling choice of homemade desserts, most often a melt-in-your-mouth *flan* that actually made my friend Brian's eyes tear up after his first bite. She took simple ingredients and, like magic, would turn them into gold.

I ate so many meals at her house, that it's hard for me to tell the difference
15 between the holiday meals she'd serve and the normal middle-of-the-week meals. Every day was a feast day at Mimi's house. My American friends have feasts on holidays, and the rest of the year they eat quickly on their way from doing one thing to doing some other thing. But the shared meal at Mimi's house—usually around 1:00 P.M.—was the whole point of the day.
20 Amazingly there was hardly any food in Mimi's cupboards or refrigerator. Everything she needed she bought each day fresh at the *bodega* on the corner as soon as it opened. She cooked it that morning, served it that afternoon, and sent leftovers to family and friends in the neighborhood. I would eat the last bits as a late-night snack with crackers and a cold glass of milk.
25 If you ever have the opportunity to eat with Cubans, at least in my family, there are two rules you should know: First, it's not enough to say you like the food—you have to prove it by cleaning your plate. That's hard because the portions are huge. Then you have to ask for a complete second helping[1] and eat that as well. But don't go for thirds or they'll call you a pig.

Antonio Sacre

[1] **helping:** an amount of food that someone serves or takes

30 The second thing is that you're not allowed to leave the table until the oldest person has left the table. It could take a long time to eat two helpings of everything Mimi prepared, especially since Nina, 83 years old and the oldest in the family, would chew her food 50 times like they taught her in Havana. When the elders would finally decide it was time to get up, you were too full to do anything else. I usually could
35 move just enough to get to the soft leather couches in the living room and collapse[2] into them. Then Mimi would come out with coffee and dessert—a tray covered with little *tazitas* of *café Cubano* and a little plate of *burrones*, Cuban cookies.

What I am really asking for when I request one of my grandmother's meals is the memory of her hugs, the smells of her kitchen, the sound of the loud laughter after the
40 meal, and the feeling of quiet, unshakable love that filled me completely whenever I was around her. She turned simple dishes of meat, beans, and rice—that for 23 years of my life nourished my body—into a meal that just the memory of now, nine years after her death, nourishes my soul.

[2] **collapse:** fall down

 **End time** _____

8 PROCESS WHAT YOU READ

Mark the answers true (T) or false (F) without looking back at the story. Then check your answers on page 132. Follow the instructions for recording your comprehension score and reading speed on the inside back cover.

____ **1.** Antonio's grandmother was an excellent cook.

____ **2.** Antonio's American friends feast every day of the year.

____ **3.** Antonio's grandmother went shopping for food once a week.

____ **4.** Antonio says that when you eat with Cubans, you should always ask for a second helping.

____ **5.** According to Antonio, it's a Cuban custom for elders to leave the table last.

9 WORK WITH THE VOCABULARY

Work with a partner. Find each italicized Spanish word in the story and highlight the context clue that explains its meaning. Compare answers with your classmates.

A. Look at the cartoon and answer the questions below. Discuss your ideas with your classmates.

"How many thousand do you figure you've eaten?"

1. What is this cartoon saying about fast food?

2. This cartoon was drawn in 1973. How do you think things have changed since then?

B. Put a check (✓) next to the words you know. Ask your classmates for the meanings of the words you don't know. Look up the words no one knows in a dictionary.

___ familiar   ___ interior   ___ oppose   ___ promote

___ quality   ___ rediscover   ___ regional   ___ treat (v.)

C. Preview the two texts on pages 76–78. Then answer these questions.

1. What types of texts are these?

2. What is the topic of each text?

3. What do you think you will learn about these topics?

D. Choose one text to read. Read the first paragraph and complete these sentences.

1. The title of my text is . . .

2. The main idea of the first paragraph is . . .

3. I found the main idea in sentence . . .

4. One detail that supports the main idea is . . .

E. As you read your text, underline the main ideas of each paragraph.

Fast-food restaurants have become a big part of American culture. This magazine article discusses the history of their success.

The Fast Growth of Fast-Food Restaurants

There are fast-food restaurants almost everywhere in the United States. There may be a McDonald's on one corner, a Kentucky Fried
5 Chicken across the street, and a Subway, Wendy's, Burger King, and Carl's Jr. just down the road. These restaurants have become a big part of American culture. They have
10 changed the way people eat and the way American cities and towns look, and it all began with two brothers who had one big idea.

In 1948 Richard and Maurice
15 McDonald decided to improve their drive-in restaurant in Southern California. They wanted to find ways to make food faster and sell it for less. First they made their menu
20 smaller, keeping only items like hamburgers and french fries. Then they used an assembly line to make and serve the food: one person made the hamburger; another put on the
25 condiments (ketchup, mustard, and pickles) and wrapped it; and a third person served it. The restaurant was instantly popular and entrepreneurs from all over the country came to
30 see the first fast-food restaurant. They were surprised by what they saw: lines of customers waiting to get in. Hoping for the same success, these businesspeople opened their
35 own fast-food restaurants.

When salesman Ray Kroc visited the McDonald brothers' restaurant, he saw more than a restaurant—he saw a gold mine, a chance to get
40 rich! Kroc convinced the McDonalds to sell him the right to franchise McDonald's Famous Hamburgers. Franchising allowed other businesspeople to open their
45 own McDonald's restaurants and to use the McDonald's name, recipes, and system of making and delivering the food. Franchises were just as popular as fast food, and soon
50 McDonald's restaurants opened all over the country. Once again, entrepreneurs knew a good idea when they saw it, and other fast-food restaurants began franchising, too.
55 In franchised fast-food restaurants, the new restaurant owners had to learn how to cook the same food and how to treat customers in exactly the same way.
60 All the restaurant buildings and interior decoration had to be the same, too. This uniformity was a key to the success of fast-food restaurant chains.[1] Anywhere in the
65 country, customers can find the comfort of the same menu, the same food, the same paint colors on the walls, and in many cases, even the same size and shape of building.
70 Wherever people go, they can walk into their favorite fast-food restaurant and feel right at home.

Is this a good thing? It depends on whom you ask. While some

---

[1] **chain:** a number of restaurants or stores owned by the same company

travelers like the comfort of eating at a familiar fast-food restaurant, others say that American cities and towns have lost their unique[2] look. Whereas fast food is a favorite of some, others feel that it is too homogeneous.[3] Now, 90 percent of American food is made from only 30 products.

To respond to the negative feelings, fast-food restaurants are working hard to change their images. Some are building new restaurants that are similar in appearance to the buildings nearby. Others are offering more diverse menus that include items like salads or regional specialties. The restaurant owners hope these changes will make their restaurants appealing to more Americans and help their businesses grow.

Whether you call fast food a curse,[4] or praise it as a convenience and a comfort, it's probably here to stay. Consider this: In 1948 there was one fast-food restaurant in the United States. By the beginning of the 21st century there were 228,000. Fast food grew—fast!

[2] **unique:** unlike anything else
[3] **homogeneous:** of the same or similar kind
[4] **curse:** something that causes great harm

12 READ B

The Slow Food movement started as a reaction to the many fast-food restaurants. This brochure tells the history and purpose of the organization Slow Food USA.

Fast Food? 🐌 Slow It Down!

Slow Food USA is an organization that supports, celebrates, and protects the food traditions of North America. Slow Food USA's goal is to rediscover the pleasure and quality in everyday life, to slow down and appreciate the traditional ways of producing, preparing, and eating food. Slow Food supports ecological[1] food production, local organic[2] farming, and regional, seasonal[3] cooking. It opposes the growth of the fast-food industry and discourages buying mass-produced[4] food products.

The History of Slow Food
Founded in Italy by Carlo Petrini in 1986, Slow Food now has 70,000 members in 45 countries. Petrini started the organization when a McDonald's restaurant opened on the historic Piazza di Spagna in Rome. He was afraid that fast food would make all cultures the same. "I wanted to slow down the fast life," Petrini said, "which changes our habits, comes into the privacy of our homes, and forces us to eat fast food."

"A generation of children thinks dinner comes out of the freezer and goes in the microwave. They don't smell it until they're at the table. That's a major change in our culture." —Jon White, cheesemaker

[1] **ecological:** safe for the environment
[2] **organic:** grown without using pesticides or other chemicals
[3] **seasonal:** happening at a particular time of year. Seasonal food is only available in the season that it grows.
[4] **mass-produced:** made in extremely large quantities, usually in a factory

Our goal is to celebrate food—Join us!!

Slow Food USA values the great diversity in the foods of North America—from the spicy Cajun
25 cooking of New Orleans, to the rich tradition of the Southwest, which mixes Western, Native American, and Mexican cuisine. It encourages farmers to grow special varieties of fruits and vegetables and to keep making products such as
30 cheeses and jams. Today, in this age of mass production, we could easily lose these foods and the farms that produce them.

Slow Food wants to:
- protect the land for today and the future.
35 - recognize that people and the environment[5] depend on each other.
- promote local, seasonal, and organically grown food.
- recognize that food expresses cultural
40 diversity.
- preserve the traditions of the table.
- improve a sense of community.

"The end of the family meal is a tragedy. The most important part of the meal isn't the food. It's that we sit down together, we stop and pay attention to each other, and we talk."
–Ruth Reichl, author, food critic

Join Slow Food USA in changing the trend of "fast" living.

Stop eating in your car or at your desk. Enjoy delicious foods at your kitchen or dining room table. Rediscover the wonderful flavors of fresh, organically grown produce. Stop to savor and
45 enjoy these foods as you gather with your family and friends to dine.

Is it difficult for you to slow down?

It's easy to convince ourselves that we don't have time, but we often let time pass by without making any real use of it.
50 Instead of wasting your time, take control by turning off the television and planting a vegetable garden, cooking your favorite dish, or sitting down for a long, relaxed meal.

Why should you slow down?

55 Research shows people who eat slowly are more likely to lose excess weight or maintain a normal weight.

People who have meals with their families report more satisfaction in their
60 everyday lives.

55 Slow Food USA has more than 70 local groups in 36 states. You can find the one nearest you on the Internet.

"If you think back across your entire life, think of the top ten happiest moments. I bet you nine out of ten of them were spent around a table with the people you love." –Kurt Friese, Restauranteur

Adapted from the Slow Food USA website

[5] **environment:** nature, the world in which we live

13 SHARE WHAT YOU LEARNED

A. Work with a partner who read the same text.

   1. Read the focus questions for your text in the chart below.

   2. Discuss the questions and write the answers.

Focus Questions for Text A
1. How did fast food get started?
2. How did fast food spread in the United States?
3. How has fast food affected the United States?
4. What are fast-food restaurants doing to help their businesses grow?

Focus Questions for Text B
1. Why did Slow Food get started?
2. Why does Slow Food USA encourage farmers to grow special varieties of fruits and vegetables?
3. How does "slowing down" affect people? Name three ways.
4. Why does the brochure use quotes? What do the quotes tell you?

B. With your partner, find a pair who read a different text and form a team.

   1. Share the topic of your text with your teammates.

   2. Take turns sharing the answers to the focus questions.

   3. Add any other information from the text you remember.

14 SHARE WHAT YOU THINK

Discuss these questions with your teammates. Then share your answers with the class.

1. Do you think fast food is a curse or a convenience? Why?

2. Does the uniformity of fast food and fast food restaurants comfort you? Why or Why not?

3. What are the differences between a "fast-food lifestyle" and a "slow food lifestyle"? Support your ideas with examples from the readings.

4. Do you have a fast-food or slow food lifestyle? Why?

5. Which lifestyle is more appealing to you or your friends? Why?

Interview

A. Read the questions and think about your answers. Then interview a partner.

1. Where do you shop for food? Why?

2. Do you like to cook? Why or why not?

3. What do you do more often: cook at home or go out for dinner? Why?

B. With your partner, discuss the advantages and disadvantages of a) using prepared foods and b) buying all the ingredients and putting them together yourself.

Chart

A. Compare mealtime customs in the U.S. and another culture that you know. Write a list of items that represent mealtime in each culture. Using your lists, follow the model to create a Venn diagram. Put items that are common to both cultures in the "Both" section.

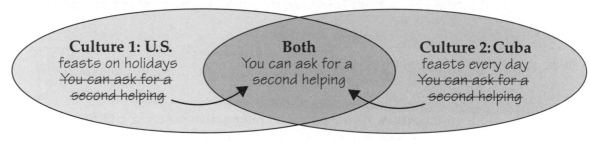

Culture 1: U.S.
feasts on holidays
~~You can ask for a second helping~~

Both
You can ask for a second helping

Culture 2: Cuba
feasts every day
~~You can ask for a second helping~~

B. Share your diagram with your classmates and discuss the similarities and differences between different cultures.

Write

Refer to the web diagram you made on page 72, section 6, exercise A to help you write one or more paragraphs about a special meal you remember. Use the answers to the questions below to add more information to your paragraphs.

• What did you do while you were eating? (talk, listen to music, etc.)

• How did you feel during the meal?

• How does the memory of it make you feel now?

Research

Read more about the topic of food.

• Use the Internet or an encyclopedia to look up *fast food, slow food,* or *comfort food.*

• Read and take notes on one or more sections of an article you find.

• Bring your notes to class and report on the information you found.

Unit 6

Consumer Awareness

In this unit you will:

● read about consumer rights and advertising in the U.S.
● learn how to summarize what you read

WHAT DO YOU KNOW ABOUT CONSUMER RIGHTS?

A. Look at the picture. Describe what happened. What can the man do about it? Discuss your ideas with your classmates.

B. Think about these questions. Discuss your answers with a partner. Then share your ideas with your classmates.

1. Have you ever bought a product that didn't work the way the advertisements said it would? What did you do about it? What was the result of your action?

2. Do you or your friends ever buy things from catalogs or the Internet? Do the products usually match their descriptions or advertisements? Give examples.

1 GET READY TO READ ABOUT: The Consumer Movement

A. Guess which statements in the chart are true. Check your guesses after you read the article on pages 84–85.

Statement	True	False
1. The consumer movement started in the early 1800s.		
2. Unsafe products and false advertising are two consumer problems.		
3. The U.S. government tries to protect consumers.		
4. Consumer protection laws protect businesses.		
5. Consumers should follow the instructions that come with the products they buy.		
6. Writers played a big role in the history of consumer rights.		
7. Some books led to consumer protection laws.		
8. When people get hurt using a product, there is nothing they can do about it.		

B. Read the following paragraph and pay attention to the underlined words. Then read the sentences below and guess which word or phrase best completes each one. Check your guesses after you read the article on pages 84–85.

> *Consumer Rights*
>
> As consumer <u>awareness</u> grows, more people are learning what their rights as buyers are. Customers now know that they can <u>complain</u> about the poor <u>quality</u> of products they buy. When a product is <u>unsatisfactory</u>, people can <u>demand</u> their money back. A company with good <u>business practices</u> will usually be happy to return the money. However, it is the customer's <u>responsibility</u> to bring the product back to the store with a receipt. A business can't always <u>control</u> how good their products are, but they can control their service to their customers.

1. Awareness is (knowledge/lack of knowledge) of something.

2. When customers complain, they usually (like/don't like) a product.

3. The quality of a product is how (good/expensive) it is.

4. An unsatisfactory product is (good/bad).

5. When people demand something they make a (strong/weak) request.

6. Business practices are (the way/the reason) a company runs.

7. A responsibility is something a person (must do/must not do).

8. When managers control businesses they (have/don't have) power over them.

82   Unit 6

A **summary** of a text is a short version that includes only the most important information. Different readers may summarize the same text differently and may use their own words in combination with the author's.

To summarize a paragraph:

- underline the main idea
- note the supporting details
- use the main idea as the basis of your summary
- add any supporting details that explain the main idea

Practice Summarizing a Paragraph

A. Read the paragraph and the notes one student wrote in the margins. Answer the questions below. Check your answers with a partner.

Upton Sinclair

1900s

Upton Sinclair wrote books about some unacceptable business practices in the United States. His books were novels, but they told true stories about unclean and dangerous conditions in the factories of the early 1900s. In his most famous book *The Jungle*, he made people aware of problems in meat-packing plants. Sinclair was an excellent writer.

novels

Unclean + dangerous conditions

meat-packing plants   "The Jungle"

1. According to the student, what is the main idea? Do you agree? Why or why not?

2. Did the student make notes on all the supporting details? Why or why not?

B. Read these summaries the student wrote. Discuss the questions below with a partner.

a. In the early 1900s, Upton Sinclair wrote novels about unclean and dangerous conditions in U.S. meat-packing plants and other factories.
b. Upton Sinclair wrote excellent books about the dangerous conditions in American factories in the early 1900s.

1. Did the student use all the information in the notes to write the summaries? Why or why not?

2. Which of the summaries is the most effective? Why?

3. If you write a summary of the same paragraph, will it be different from these? How?

Use Your Reading Skills

A. Preview the article below and read the first paragraph. Then discuss these questions with your classmates.

1. What is the topic of this article?

2. What do you already know about the topic?

3. What do you think you will learn about the topic?

4. What is the main idea of the first paragraph?

5. What is one supporting detail?

B. Scan the article for dates. Use the dates you find and the information around them to make a timeline of the consumer movement in the U.S. For example, your first item would be:

1890—Sherman Act

3 READ

The protection of consumers—people who buy products and services—is a major concern in the U.S. This encyclopedia article examines the history of the consumer movement and its role today.

THE CONSUMER MOVEMENT

The consumer movement in the United States began in the early 1900s. Since then, it has protected buyers from unfair business practices, such as selling
5 unsafe products; false advertising, labeling, or packaging; and actions that decrease competition.[1]

The consumer movement has an interesting history. At the beginning of
10 the 20th century, manufacturers were selling many unclean and unsafe items, so consumers wanted laws to control product quality. Authors called *muckrakers* wrote about wrongdoings by various companies.
15 A famous example, Upton Sinclair's *The Jungle* (1906), described the unclean conditions in the meat-packing industry.

This book led to the U.S. Pure Food and Drug Act of 1906, which controlled
20 the preparation and production of foods and medicines.

Around the same time, there were some large companies that had no competition from other businesses.
25 Therefore, they were able to monopolize, or control, the supply of many products and charge high prices for them. Since cheaper products were unavailable, customers had to buy the expensive
30 items. To fight monopolies, Congress passed the Sherman Act in 1890.

Yet another problem for consumers came with the rapid growth of business and industry. Companies began to

[1] **competition:** a situation in which more than one company is in the same type of business

35 advertise much more, and sometimes the ads made false claims[2] about products. As a result, consumer groups began to fight for complete and truthful product information. In response, in 1914 the new
40 Federal Trade Commission began to control advertising. Another victory came in 1929 with the start of Consumers' Research, Inc., a service that provided product testing and evaluation.

45   During the 1950s and 1960s, once again several writers called attention to consumer issues. Vance Packard's books, *The Hidden Persuaders* (1957) and *The Wastemakers* (1960) identified some
50 types of advertising that tried to make people buy products they didn't need. Another example was Ralph Nader's *Unsafe at Any Speed* (1965), about safety problems in certain automobiles.
55 His book led to the National Traffic and Motor Vehicle Safety Act of 1966.

    The 1970s and 1980s were a time of even greater consumer awareness and activism.[3] For example, during the 1970s,
60 the high cost of living pushed up the prices of some products. The consumer movement organized large groups of people to stop buying beef, sugar, and coffee, and this resulted in lower prices
65 for a while. In the 1980s, more public concern about health led to a demand for nutritional information on food packaging.

    Currently, consumer groups and government agencies work to protect the
70 rights of consumers to have:
- products whose quality matches their prices and the claims of manufacturers.
- protection against unsafe products.
- truthful, complete information about
75 products or services.
- a choice among a variety of products.
- the right to complain about unsatisfactory products and services and get compensation[4] when there is a
80 good reason for the complaint.

    Along with rights, consumers also have some responsibilities. For example, they should follow the instructions that come with a product and use it correctly.
85   Today, consumer groups and government agencies play an even greater role in consumer protection. They gather and share information about almost every type of product and service. They also
90 provide advice about the most effective ways to get compensation for broken products or bad service. Thanks to the consumer movement, buyers now have a great deal of useful information to guide
95 them, a big choice of products, and the strong support of a wide variety of consumer protection laws.

Adapted from the *World Book Encyclopedia*

[2] **claim:** a statement that something is true
[3] **activism:** taking action with the goal of political or social change
[4] **compensation:** payment to a buyer for a bad product or poor service

4 PROCESS WHAT YOU READ

A. Answer these questions. Then discuss your answers with a partner. Look back at the article to check your answers.

1. Why did the consumer movement get started?

2. Which authors contributed to the consumer movement? What did they do?

3. What are monopolies? How did the government try to control them?

4. Why did advertising need government control?

5. What are the rights of consumers?

6. What are the responsibilities of consumers?

B. Reread paragraphs 3, 4, and 6 in the article on pages 84–85 and choose a heading for each one below. Then write your own headings for paragraphs 7 and 8. Share you answers with the class. Discuss why some headings are better than others.

Paragraph 3

  a. No Competition   b. Fighting Monopolies   c. The Sherman Act

Paragraph 4

  a. Federal Trade   b. Advertising   c. Controlling Advertising
     Commission Begins

Paragraph 6

  a. Consumer Activism   b. 1970s and 1980s   c. A Demand for Information
     Grows

C. Think about these questions. Discuss your answers with your classmates.

1. How has the consumer movement changed the way companies do business in the United States? How has it changed consumers' attitudes toward products and companies?

2. How do you think business owners feel about consumer protection laws? How do you think the consumers feel about these laws? Why?

D. Reread the following excerpt from the article on pages 84–85. Summarize the paragraph in one sentence. Use the bulleted steps on page 83 to help you. Share your summary with your classmates.

> During the 1950s and 1960s, once again several writers called attention to consumer issues. Vance Packard's books, *The Hidden Persuaders* (1957) and *The Wastemakers* (1960) identified some types of advertising that tried to make people buy products they didn't need. Another example was Ralph Nader's *Unsafe at Any Speed* (1965) about safety problems in certain automobiles.

5 WORK WITH THE VOCABULARY

A. Match the words with their definitions. Then write a sentence for each word.

_____ **1.** complain   a. make a strong request for something

_____ **2.** quality   b. knowledge or understanding

_____ **3.** control   c. say that you're unhappy about something

_____ **4.** demand   d. a duty or job

_____ **5.** awareness   e. how good or bad something is

_____ **6.** responsibility   f. to have power over something

B. Choose the correct adjective in each sentence.

1. Upton Sinclair wrote about (acceptable/unacceptable) conditions at meat-packing plants. His books helped conditions change and become more (acceptable/unacceptable).

2. It is important for food to be (clean/unclean) and pure. (Clean/Unclean) food can cause disease.

3. In the early 1900s, customers had to pay high prices for the products that were (available/unavailable). Because of monopolies, cheaper products were (available/unavailable).

4. It was (fair/unfair) for companies to keep other companies from selling similar products. Laws now require companies to allow (fair/unfair) competition.

5. Before the 1960s some cars were (safe/unsafe). The National Traffic and Motor Vehicle Safety Act required manufacturers to produce (safe/unsafe) cars.

6. (Truthful/Untruthful) product advertising is against the law. Companies must give consumers (truthful/untruthful) product information.

7. Customers should return (broken/unbroken) products to the store. Stores will replace them with (broken/unbroken) items or give a refund.

8. When a product hurts someone or is (satisfactory/unsatisfactory), the customer can complain. If there's a good reason for the complaint, the customer should get (satisfactory/unsatisfactory) compensation.

C. Scan the article on pages 84–85 for the words *monopolize* and *muckrakers*. Highlight the context clues in the article that explain the meanings. Check your answers with a partner.

A. **Look at the drawing and answer the questions below. Discuss your ideas with your classmates.**

1. What is wrong with the car?

2. What do you think the sign means?

B. **Put a check (✓) next to the words or phrases you know. Ask your classmates for the meanings of the ones you don't know. Look up the words and phrases no one knows in a dictionary.**

___ electrical	___ eligible	___ fed up with	___ figure out
___ in luck	___ reasonable	___ repair (n.)	___ take advantage of

Use Your Reading Skills

A. **Preview the article on pages 89–90. Work with a partner to answer these questions.**

1. What type of article is this?

2. What is the topic of the article?

3. What do you already know about the topic?

4. What do you predict you will learn from this article?

B. **Read the article quickly, skipping any words you don't know. Time your reading. Put the start time at the top and the end time at the bottom. Then answer the questions on page 90, section 8.**

🕐 **Start time** _____

Advice columns are popular in the United States. In this column, a new car owner asks for information about his rights as a consumer.

Ask Mr. Fix It

Dear Mr. Fix It,
I bought a new car nine months ago and it has been nothing but
5 trouble. In the first month, the car started having electrical problems, so I took it back to the car dealer.[1] It was in the repair shop there for
10 more than a week. Then the radio blew up and I needed to replace it. Three weeks ago, the electrical problems started again. I took the car back to the dealer for repair, and it has been there ever since. At first the
15 mechanic didn't know what was wrong with it, but now he says my "new" car needs a new engine. I think my car is a lemon[2] and I'm fed up with all these problems. Is there anything I can do to get
20 rid of this car and get my money back?

New Car Blues
New York

Dear New Car Blues,
You're in luck! Every state in the Union[3]
25 has a "lemon law" that protects consumers in your situation. The law says that car dealers or manufacturers must fix new vehicles with serious defects[4] after a reasonable number of tries. If they can't fix
30 it, they must replace the car or refund your money. An arbitrator[5] decides whether or not you are eligible for a refund.

In your state, New York, you can figure out if your new car is a lemon by answering
35 these questions:

1. Does the car still have a problem after it has been in the repair shop at least four times for the same repair?

2. Has the car been in the repair shop for a
40 total of 30 or more days for any problems, and does the car still have these problems?

For more information or assistance, look at the many lemon law websites on the Internet.

45 Good luck!
Mr. Fix It

Dear Readers:
Here's some information about the lemon law, one of the most important consumer
50 protection laws. It has been in effect for more than 20 years in some states. The fight for this kind of protection started in Southern California when Rosemary Shahan purchased a new car that had many
55 problems. Ms. Shahan was very angry because the mechanics were unable to fix her car after many tries. She asked for her money back but the dealer wouldn't give it to her. To protest this unsatisfactory service
60 and the problems with her car, Ms. Shahan stood outside the car dealership for five months with a sign that said, "My car is a lemon." Many people stopped to tell her stories about their lemon cars and she

---

[1] **dealer:** someone who buys and sells a certain type of product
[2] **lemon:** something that turns out to be unsatisfactory
[3] **the Union:** the United States of America
[4] **defect:** something wrong
[5] **arbitrator:** a person who is chosen to settle an argument between two opposing sides

65 realized she was not alone. Newspapers and television news programs reported her story and Ms. Shahan contacted legislators[6] to help her. Together they were able to create the first lemon law in the United States.

70 Many states have lemon laws for used cars, too. Now some states are planning to write lemon laws for new homes, computers, and other consumer items. So the next time you have a serious problem with a product, check 75 to see if you can get help by taking advantage of the many laws that protect consumers.

Until next time,
Mr. Fix It

[6] **legislator:** an elected government official who participates in making laws

 **End time** _____

8 PROCESS WHAT YOU READ

Mark the statements true (T) or false (F) without looking back at the article. Check your answers on page 133. Follow the instructions for recording your comprehension score and reading speed on the inside back cover.

____ 1. "New Car Blues" thinks his car is a lemon.

____ 2. New York has a lemon law.

____ 3. Rosemary Shahan got the first lemon law passed all by herself.

____ 4. Lemon laws began in New York.

____ 5. Some states plan to have lemon laws for other products.

9 WORK WITH THE VOCABULARY

Choose the correct word or phrase to complete the sentences below. Check your answers with a partner. Then with your partner, write a new sentence for each word or phrase.

a. eligible	b. fed up with	c. figure out
d. in luck	e. reasonable	f. take advantage of

1. When you find a good mechanic, you are ____.

2. A mechanic should be able to fix your car in a ____ amount of time.

3. Sometimes it's hard to ____ what's wrong with a car.

4. When the mechanic can't fix the problem, it's easy to get ____ the car.

5. Sometimes you can ____ the consumer protection laws.

6. If the repair takes too long, you may be ____ for a refund.

10 GET READY TO READ AND SHARE

A. In a small group, use the chart to categorize the following ideas about advertising. Explain why you think the ideas are positive, negative, or interesting. Then add some of your own ideas to the chart.

> *Ads are memorable.*
>
> *Ads tell people about new products.*
>
> *Americans see 3,000 ads each day.*
>
> *Company names are often on clothing.*

ADVERTISING		
Positive	**Negative**	**Interesting**
Ads tell people about new products.		

B. Put a check (✓) next to the words that you know. Ask a partner for the meanings of the words you don't know. Look up the words no one knows in a dictionary.

____ commercial(n.)   ____ estimate(v.)   ____ ignore   ____ influence(n.)

____ interrupt   ____ satisfy   ____ slogan   ____ volunteering

C. Preview the two texts on pages 92–94. Then answer these questions.

1. What is the topic of each text?

2. What do you already know about the topics?

D. Choose one text to read. Read the first paragraph and complete these sentences.

1. The title of my text is . . .

2. The main idea of the first paragraph is . . .

3. I predict I will learn . . .

E. Preview the focus questions for your text on page 95. As you read, highlight the answers to the questions.

American life is full of advertisements that encourage a desire to have things. This magazine article explains the power of advertising in the United States.

WHY WE BUY

HOW do people in the United States decide what to buy? Research has shown that one of the most important influences on buying habits is
5 advertising. Memorable ads with colorful pictures and catchy slogans are a familiar part of everyday life. They appear in print, on television, and in the movies. Advertising is
10 hard to ignore, but different people respond to it in different ways.

ADVERTISING IS EVERYWHERE

As people walk or drive along the street, ads for the newest products
15 scream out from billboards and buildings, train platforms, and bus shelters. Even buses are often covered with ads inside and out. Magazines and newspapers are full of ads for
20 products and services. Commercials interrupt television programs every 8–10 minutes. At the movies, there is at least 15 minutes of advertising for products, services, and other movies
25 before the film begins. There is also a type of advertising, called product placement, in movies and on TV. For example, a performer may drink a brand-name soda, eat at a well-known
30 chain restaurant, or drive away in a stylish car. With product placement, the audience can read company names on the various products they

see. Ads in the form of logos[1] are even
35 on clothing. It's difficult to get away from advertising. Like it or not, messages to buy things bombard[2] Americans almost all the time. Media expert, Mark Landler, estimates that
40 people in the United States see 3,000 advertisements every day.

TV shows and advertisements have a great influence on people, according to economist and author, Juliet B.
45 Schor. "In a study I found that people spent about $208 more a year on purchases for each hour of TV they watched a week. For example, people who watched about 11 1/2 hours of
50 TV a week spent $2,400 a year more than they would have if they turned off their TVs."

THE PSYCHOLOGY OF ADVERTISING

55 Advertising tries to convince people that buying things will satisfy some important emotional needs. In his article, "Why the Self Is Empty," psychologist Phillip Cushman
60 explains that, over time, people in the United States have become more isolated. Many of them live alone or far away from their families, and they don't feel part of a community.
65 These feelings of isolation and

[1] **logo:** a symbol that represents a company or organization
[2] **bombard:** to give too much of something, without stopping

emptiness make the "good life" as shown in advertising—a life full of things—seem very desirable.

A Different Response

70 Some Americans try not to respond to advertising. They turn off their TVs, and they stay away from malls and shopping catalogs. "Studies show that during a six year period, 75 19 percent of Americans downshifted, choosing to work less, earn less, and spend less. They say that being with their families is more important than buying the latest things and earning 80 lots of money," writes Juliet Schor. The Center for a New American Dream supports people who want to be responsible consumers. This organization encourages people to 85 buy only what they need; it discourages shopping to satisfy emotional needs.

Still, advertising is hard to ignore. U.S. companies spend over $200 90 billion a year on it. One company might spend $300,000 to produce a short TV commercial and another $300,000 to broadcast it. Companies know that advertising works. They 95 want it to be a powerful influence on consumers, and many succeed. With all the money advertisers spend, it's no surprise that advertising is such a big part of life. No wonder we buy!

12 READ B

Advertising is a powerful tool that can sell ideas as well as products. This article introduces the Ad Council, an organization that uses advertising to sell ideas that affect how Americans think and behave.

| File | Edit | View | Tools | Help | _ □ × |

◄ Back   ► Forward   ⊗ Stop   ⇄ Refresh   🏠 Home

Advertising for Ideas

"Just say no." "Only you can prevent forest fires." These slogans are the work of the Ad Council, whose mission[1] is to sell ideas to the American public. This organization uses media such as television and radio commercials, posters, and billboards to make 5 people aware of social, environmental, and health problems. The Ad Council creates public service announcements (PSAs) to talk about the importance of volunteering, cleaning up the environment, avoiding drugs, and other key issues. PSAs have two main goals: to inform the public and to help people change their behavior.

[1] **mission:** a special job or task

Changing Behavior

10　The Ad Council has played an important role in the
United States since 1942. Its slogans and characters have
educated, influenced, and inspired[2] generations. One of its
most memorable characters is Smokey Bear,[3] a brown bear
dressed as a forest ranger. Smokey gives tips on fire safety
15　and tells campers, "Only you can prevent forest fires."
Americans began hearing this slogan in 1944, and most
people still recognize it today. Since the start of the
campaign,[4] the number of forest fires caused by campers has
decreased dramatically, and the number of acres lost to fire has gone from 22 million to
20　4 million per year. The Smokey Bear Forest Fire Prevention campaign is one of the
longest-running, most famous, and most effective public service advertising campaigns
in U.S. history.

Smokey Bear

Saving Lives

The Ad council also created a very successful seat belt campaign. When seat belts
25　were first available in the 1960s, most Americans gave excuses for not wearing them.
They said the seat belts were annoying or too much trouble, or that the belts would
wrinkle their clothing. To convince people to wear seat belts, the Ad council designed a
campaign that featured two crash test dummies. In the ads the
dummies, Vince and Larry, got badly hurt in a car crash
30　because they weren't wearing seat belts. The Ad Council's
slogan warned the public, "You can learn alot from a dummy…
Buckle your safety belt." Vince and Larry became well-known
figures in American popular culture, and millions of people
took their message to heart. The Crash Test Dummies campaign
35　began in 1985, and since then, safety belt usage has increased from 21% to 73%. The
Council estimates that this campaign has saved 85,000 lives.

Crash Test Dummies
Vince and Larry

Making It Happen

One organization alone cannot do such important work. The Ad Council teams up
with others who contribute their time and expertise to the public service ad campaigns.
40　Experienced marketing[5] executives help the Ad Council identify their audience and
decide how best to reach them. Top advertising agencies help create the ads. Once the
ads are completed, they run free of charge on TV and radio.

Working together with these groups, the Ad Council sends out important messages
to the American public. Through powerful images and words, public service
45　announcements influence the way Americans think. This in turn, can change millions
of American lives.

---

[2] **inspire:** to give someone a feeling of wanting to do something good
[3] Many Americans call this character Smokey "the" Bear, but his real name is Smokey Bear.
[4] **campaign:** a plan for a series of organized actions for a specific purpose
[5] **marketing:** the part of business that decides how a product can be sold most effectively

13 SHARE WHAT YOU LEARNED

A. Work with a partner who read the same text.

1. Read the focus questions for your text in the chart below.

2. Discuss the questions and write the answers.

FOCUS QUESTIONS FOR TEXT A
1. Name three types of advertising.
2. How does advertising influence people?
3. According to Phillip Cushman, why do Americans respond to advertising?
4. Why do U.S. companies spend a lot of money on advertising?

FOCUS QUESTIONS FOR TEXT B
1. What does the Ad Council do? Why?
2. What was the result of the Smokey Bear campaign?
3. What impact did the seat belt campaign have on Americans?
4. How does the Ad Council produce PSAs?

B. With your partner, find a pair who read a different text and form a team.

1. Share the topic of your text with your teammates.

2. Take turns sharing the answers to the focus questions.

3. Add any other information from the text you remember.

14 SHARE WHAT YOU THINK

Discuss these questions with your teammates. Then share your answers with the class.

1. What are the advantages and disadvantages of advertising?

2. Describe two advertisements that you've seen—one for a product and one for an idea. Were they effective or ineffective? Why?

3. What makes you buy a product? What makes you believe in an idea? Explain.

4. How do you think advertising affects U.S culture? How does advertising affect other cultures that you know?

15 REFLECT ON WHAT YOU READ IN THIS UNIT

Interview

Read the questions and think about your answers. Then interview a partner. With your partner, decide whether the government should control advertising, and if so, in what ways.

1. Name two advertised products that you like to buy. Why do you choose them over other products?

2. Which advertisements make you feel good? Which ones make you feel bad? Explain.

Write

Write a two-sentence summary of a section of the article you read on pages 92–94.

- For *Why We Buy*, summarize "The Psychology of Advertising."

- For *Advertising for Ideas* summarize "Saving Lives."

Use the bulleted steps on page 83 to help you. Compare your summary with a partner who read the same article. Then share your summary with the class.

16 REFLECT ON YOUR READING STRATEGIES

A. Read the questions in the chart and choose the answers that best describe your use of the reading strategies. Then with your classmates, discuss which strategies are the most helpful.

Strategy	How often do you use this strategy outside of this class?			How helpful is this strategy?		
	Always	Sometimes	Never	Very	A little	Not
Previewing and predicting						
Scanning						
Skipping Words						
Using context clues						
Finding the main idea						
Summarizing						

B. Tell a partner which strategies are the easiest for you and which strategies you need to practice more.

Unit 7

Extreme Sports

In this unit you will:

● **read about extreme sports in the U.S.**
● **learn how to skim a text**
● **learn more about reading speed**

WHAT DO YOU KNOW ABOUT EXTREME SPORTS?

A. **Look at the cartoon. Describe the people. What are they doing? What is the cartoonist's message? Discuss your ideas with your classmates.**

B. **Think about these questions. Discuss your answers with a partner. Then share your ideas with your classmates.**

1. Which sports do you think are exciting? Do you watch or participate in any of these sports? Why or why not?

2. What else do you do for fun, excitement, or adventure?

1 GET READY TO READ ABOUT: Extreme Sports

A. Read the graph and answer the questions below. Compare answers with a partner. Discuss your ideas with your classmates.

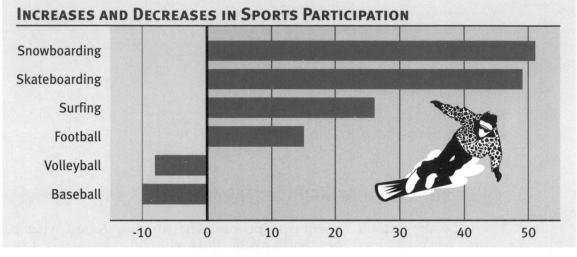

INCREASES AND DECREASES IN SPORTS PARTICIPATION

Source: American Sports Data

1. Which sports have become more popular?

2. Which sports have become less popular?

3. Why do you think interest in these sports has changed?

B. Guess the meaning of the underlined word or phrase in each sentence. Match each one with a phrase that has a similar meaning. Check your guesses after you read the article on pages 100–101.

____ **1.** Gary is an <u>athlete</u> and loves sports.

a. skill or talent

____ **2.** He has the <u>ability</u> to play sports of all kinds.

b. test of

____ **3.** He also likes excitement. It's part of his <u>personality</u>.

c. lives through

____ **4.** He likes the danger and <u>thrill</u> of extreme sports.

d. the qualities of a person that affect his or her behavior

____ **5.** Riding high ocean waves is a <u>challenge</u> to his skill as a surfer.

e. takes a chance on losing

____ **6.** When he does extreme sports, he <u>risks</u> his life.

f. gets hurt

____ **7.** When he <u>survives</u> a jump from an airplane, he feels brave.

g. a person who is good at sports

____ **8.** Sometimes he has accidents and <u>gets injuries.</u>

h. excitement

Skimming a text means moving your eyes quickly down a page, not reading every word. You can skim a text in order to:

- get an idea of what the text is about.
- decide if the text has the information you need.
- review a text after you've read it.

One way to skim is to look quickly at the first paragraph, the first sentences of each paragraph, and the last paragraph, not reading every word.

Practice Skimming

A. Preview the title of the essay below. Then practice skimming: take 25 seconds to read only the parts that are underlined.

Taking It to the Extreme!

<u>Extreme skateboarding began</u> in a California beach community in the <u>early 1970s</u>. A <u>small group of surfers</u>, bored when the surf was low, <u>started playing around with some old skateboards</u>. They <u>replaced the old wheels</u> with new urethane ones <u>to give the boards mobility and speed</u>. The <u>Z-boys</u>, named for their connection with the Zephyr Surf Shop, <u>looked for places with steep inclines</u> where they could <u>practice their surfing moves on dry land</u> until the surf came up.

Soon, the <u>Z-boys discovered that empty swimming pools provided</u> just what they needed for their <u>rides up and into the air</u>. Because of the drought in California at that time, there wasn't enough water to fill swimming pools, so the boys had plenty of empty ones. With so many places to play, the Z-boys spent hours and hours, trying new challenging moves.

The <u>Z-boys entered</u> a <u>national skateboarding contest</u> in <u>1975</u> and <u>amazed everyone</u> who saw them. The <u>Z-boys won almost all</u> the <u>events</u>. Their gravity-defying moves <u>established skateboarding as an extreme sport</u>.

B. Answer these questions without looking back at the essay. Check your answers with a partner.

1. What is the topic of the essay?

2. Imagine you have to write a paragraph on the future of skateboarding. Does this essay have the information you need?

3. What is the essay about? Choose the best answer.

   a. The Z-boys discovered empty swimming pools.
   b. A small group of surfers started the sport of extreme skateboarding.
   c. A small group of surfers invented skateboards.

Use Your Reading Skills

A. Take forty seconds to preview and skim the article below. As you skim, read only the parts that are underlined.

B. Answer these questions without looking back at the article.

    1. What is the topic of the article?

    2. In this article, will you find out why people take risks?

    3. According to the article, are extreme sports popular now? In the future will they become more or less popular?

    4. What are two other things you learned by skimming?

C. Now read the article. As you read, check your answers to the questions in part B, above.

3 READ

Why are extreme sports so popular in the U.S.? This newspaper article examines why more and more Americans are taking risks to have fun.

Taking Risks...

The <u>popularity of extreme sports</u> is <u>growing</u>, and these sports are quickly becoming <u>a part of everyday life</u>. Americans both young
5 and old are going beyond the challenges of ordinary sports and pushing themselves as far as they possibly
10 can—to the extreme. <u>Many people</u> are trying <u>extreme skateboarding</u>, <u>downhill mountain biking</u>, and <u>extreme</u>
15 <u>in-line skating</u>. Others are leaving baseball diamonds and volleyball courts to do

Extreme Skateboarding

<u>more dangerous sports like extreme</u>
20 <u>skiing and ice climbing</u>. Expert surfers ride giant 60-foot waves. Highly skilled skydivers are taking even more risks by <u>BASE jumping</u>.[1]
  <u>Why</u> are <u>people risking</u> their <u>lives</u>
25 <u>for</u> these <u>dangerous thrills</u>? Psychologist Frank Farley from Temple University says, "If you want to
30 understand America, you must know extreme sports." He points out that risk and change have
35 always played an important role in American history. The United States became a country

[1] **BASE jumping:** leaping from Buildings, Antennas, Spans (bridges), and Earth (cliffs) with a parachute

40 when citizens fought the Revolutionary War against England in order to change the government. Years later, pioneers moved west, leaving their homes and facing many
45 difficulties and risks as they began their new lives. These Americans experienced exciting challenges and threatening situations to reach their goals.

50 Psychologists have identified a certain personality type that looks for risks and thrills. Farley calls
55 these people Type T and considers the United States a Type T nation. Why? Farley views immigration to a
60 new country as very risky. He thinks that people who immigrate are often those who look for excitement
65 and adventure. Therefore, countries with many immigrants, such as the United States, have a high number of risk takers.

Type T people have a strong desire
70 to live life fully and to experience all they can. They feel more alive when they test their mental and physical abilities. Risking their lives and surviving dangerous challenges makes
75 athletes feel braver, stronger, and more self-confident,[2] and these

Ice Climbing

feelings carry over into their everyday lives. "There is nothing more empowering[3] than taking a risk and
80 succeeding," says Farley.

Taking risks also causes more injuries. In the past few years many more Americans have gone to hospital emergency rooms after
85 skateboarding, snowboarding, and mountain climbing accidents. However, despite all the injuries, the number of people
90 who participate in extreme sports keeps growing, while the number of participants in traditional sports
95 keeps declining. According to American Sports Data, Inc., in one year the number of baseball
100 players declined by 10% while the number of skateboarders and snowboarders went up by about 50%.

Frank Farley predicts that "extreme
105 sports will become the major spectator[4] and participant sports of the 21st century." Baseball, America's national pastime, "will become a minor sport," he says. "Sports that
110 involve speed, variety, and change will replace it," states Farley, because these "sports are closer to the central character of America."

[2] **self-confident:** sure of one's own abilities and value
[3] **empowering:** making someone feel in control of his or her life
[4] **spectator:** someone who watches an event such as a game

4 PROCESS WHAT YOU READ

A. In groups of four, answer the questions below. Assign each person a different question. Write the answer to your question and share it with the group.

1. Why are Americans leaving traditional sports and doing extreme sports?

2. What two examples from history show that Americans have always been risk takers? Give any other examples you know.

3. What is a Type T personality? Why is the United States a Type T nation?

4. Which other nations are Type T?

5. Why do Type T people take risks?

B. Work with a partner. Review the fourth paragraph of the article. Then write a two-sentence summary of it. Share your summary with your classmates.

5 WORK WITH THE VOCABULARY

A. Cross out the word that does not belong in each word set.

1. life-threatening	dangerous	risky	strong
2. thrills	goals	excitement	adventure
3. popular	challenging	risky	extreme
4. growing	increasing	rising	declining
5. everyday	usual	extreme	ordinary

B. Look at the words in the chart and notice their endings. Use the chart to help you complete each set of sentences below.

Action	Person	Topic
climb	climb**er**	climb**ing**

1. Famous __climber__ Mark Wellman wanted to _____ a mountain in Yosemite National Park. _____ has always been very important to Mark.

2. When people _skateboard_ they try to copy Tony Hawk. Tony Hawk is a well-known _____. _____ is his whole life.

3. _Skydiving_ was one of the first extreme sports. It isn't easy to _____. A _____ has to be very brave to jump out of an airplane.

4. People all over the world like to ___ski___. Extreme _____ is also very popular. At one time, Kristine Ulmer was the best female extreme _____ in the world.

6 IMPROVING READING SPEED: Changing Reading Speed

> A good reading practice is to change your reading speed, depending on the type of material you are reading. It's important to read complex materials, such as an article about science, more slowly than simple materials, for example an advertisement.

A. Read the list of materials and circle the ones that you think are complex. Share your ideas with a partner.

novel	short story	textbook article	comic book
TV listings	brochure	magazine article	web page
interview	letter	newspaper article	encyclopedia article
poem	sports news	advice column	biographical article

B. Think about the materials you read. Which is the most complex? Which is the simplest? How does this affect your reading speed?

7 GET READY TO READ ABOUT: BASE Jumping

A. Rate each situation in the chart to find out if you're a risk taker. Add up your points and check the key below. Then compare your responses with your classmates.

ARE YOU A RISK TAKER?				
Situation	**Rating: 1 = I dislike it very much.** **4 = I love it.**			
1. going to a new restaurant	1	2	3	4
2. traveling to new places	1	2	3	4
3. driving fast	1	2	3	4
4. riding a roller coaster	1	2	3	4
5. doing extreme sports	1	2	3	4
6. changing jobs	1	2	3	4
	Total points _____			

Key *6–10 points: You prefer to stay home.* *15–19 points: You like some adventure.*
 11–14 points: You take few risks. *20–24 points: You are definitely a risk taker!*

B. Put a (✓) next to the words you know. Ask your classmates for the meanings of the words you don't know. Look up the words no one knows in a dictionary.

____ acre   ____ ceremony   ____ design (v.)   ____ float

____ issue   ____ legal   ____ oversee   ____ parachute

Use Your Reading Skills

A. Preview the article below. Then take one minute to skim it quickly, reading the first few phrases each person says. Then answer these questions without looking back at the article. Compare answers with a partner.

1. What type of text is it?

2. What is the topic?

3. What are two things you learned by skimming?

4. Will you read more about Type T people in this article? (If you don't remember what Type T means, skim the article on pages 100–101 to review this information.)

B. Read the article quickly, skipping any words you don't know. Time your reading. Put the start time at the top and the end time at the bottom. Then answer the questions on page 106, section 9, exercise A.

8 READ

🕐 **Start time** _____

BASE jumping has become a popular extreme sport in the United States. Brenda and Dennis McGlynn love this sport so much they even got married on a jump. In this article, a sports journalist interviews the McGlynns.

BASE Jumpers 'Love' Their Sport

Sports Illustrated: Dennis, why did you and Brenda get married on a jump?

Dennis: Well, nobody has ever
5   done a BASE jump at a
    wedding, and jumping is such a
    big part of our lives that we
    wanted do it in our ceremony.

Sports Illustrated: Tell me about
10 your wedding.

Brenda: I can't believe it was three
    years ago! It was beautiful. I
    wore white satin and Dennis
    wore a black tuxedo. The
15 minister married us on the top
    of the Foresthill Bridge outside
    Auburn, California. Our guests
    climbed up the 750-foot high
    bridge with us.

Dennis McGlynn BASE Jumping

20 **Dennis:** And just after we said "I
    do" we jumped. We felt like
    birds up there.

Brenda: I think my mom was
    worried that we were going to
25 die, but after a few seconds our

parachutes opened. Mine was white and his was black. Then we had a fabulous 30-second hand-in-hand float to the ground.

Sports Illustrated: How did you two meet?

Dennis: We met when we both worked for the same sports clothing company. Brenda designed the skydiving suits and I sewed them.

Brenda: Then Dennis got into BASE jumping and I ground-crewed[1] for him. After a while I got interested in it, too.

Sports Illustrated: What's your dream jump?

Dennis: Well, we've made about 1,500 jumps, and we keep looking for something bigger and better. I think our favorite jump was six years ago, off Angel Falls in Venezuela, the world's highest waterfall.

Brenda: I also loved our jump off one of the world's tallest buildings. We jumped 88 stories in Kuala Lumpur, Malaysia, to celebrate the New Year last year.

Sports Illustrated: Recently, there has been some discussion over the legality of BASE jumping. Tell me about that.

Dennis: It's legal depending on where you do it. In the western U.S., you can do it on land that the Bureau of Land Management[2] oversees. There are about 250 million acres where we can make legal jumps. Staying within the law is important in BASE jumping.

Sports Illustrated: Why do you do this dangerous sport?

Dennis: You really have to pay attention when you do a BASE jump. If something goes wrong, you have to fix the problem. You have to rely on yourself, and doing this helps me keep my sanity.[3] I'm not worrying about anything when I'm jumping.

Sports Illustrated: Aren't you worried about your safety?

Dennis: Sure we are. That's why we design and sell BASE jumping equipment. Our company tries to make the safest equipment a jumper can get.

Brenda: Safety is the biggest issue in this sport. Since 1980, when BASE jumping started getting popular, about 45 people have died and lots of people have gotten hurt. Three years before Angel Falls, I broke my back on a jump, but a year after the accident, I was jumping again. It's so exciting, I just can't resist[4] doing it.

Dennis: We're as in love with the sport as we are with each other. It's part of who we are. ◆

Adapted from an article by Lars Anderson for *Sports Illustrated Magazine*

[1] **ground-crew** *(v):* to be responsible for the equipment and other safety details of a base jump
[2] **Bureau of Land Management:** a U.S. government agency that supervises public land
[3] **sanity:** good mental health
[4] **resist:** to stop oneself from doing something

 **End time** _____

9 PROCESS WHAT YOU READ

A. Mark these statements true (T) or false (F) without looking back at the article. Check your answers on page 134. Follow the instructions for recording your comprehension score and reading speed on the inside back cover.

____ **1.** Brenda and Dennis BASE jumped as part of their wedding.

____ **2.** The minister and the guests BASE jumped, too.

____ **3.** Brenda and Dennis met at work.

____ **4.** They have made 2,000 BASE jumps.

____ **5.** Safety is a big issue in BASE jumping.

B. Number the sentences in order. Look back at the article to check your answers.

____ Brenda and Dennis started BASE jumping.

____ They jumped from an 88-story building.

_1_ Brenda and Dennis worked at a skydiving company.

____ Brenda broke her back on a BASE jump.

____ Brenda and Dennis got married.

____ They jumped from Angel Falls in Venezuela.

10 WORK WITH THE VOCABULARY

Choose the word or phrase that has a meaning similar to the underlined word in each sentence.

____ **1.** Brenda and Dennis' wedding <u>ceremony</u> was unusual.

____ **2.** They <u>designed</u> their own clothes and equipment.

____ **3.** They even chose the color of their <u>parachutes</u>.

____ **4.** They BASE jumped on a 10-<u>acre</u> area outside Auburn, CA.

____ **5.** They <u>floated</u> slowly down from a tall bridge.

____ **6.** It was a lot of work to <u>oversee</u> the wedding.

____ **7.** Brenda and Dennis took care of every <u>issue</u> that came up.

____ **8.** Dennis made sure the jump was <u>legal</u>.

a. supervise

b. moved slowly through the air

c. measurement of land

d. permitted by law

e. an event that marks a special occasion

f. large pieces of strong cloth attached to ropes

g. topic for discussion

h. drew plans for something to be made

A. **Read the paragraph and think about the questions below. Write down your ideas. You don't have to write complete sentences. Then share your responses with your classmates.**

> ### A Boring World
>
> *Life in the United States has become boring. Everywhere you go, you find malls filled with the same stores and the same restaurants. On television or at the movies you see the same stories over and over. Extreme sports satisfy the need for excitement in a boring world.*

1. Do you think life in the U.S. is boring? Why or why not?

2. Besides the need for excitement, what other needs do extreme sports satisfy? Explain.

B. **Put a check (✓) next to the words or phrases you know. Ask your classmates for the meanings of the ones you don't know. Look up the words and phrases no one knows in a dictionary.**

____ accomplish   ____ in control

____ commitment   ____ raise (v.)

____ competence   ____ steep (adj.)

____ express oneself   ____ wheelchair

C. **Preview the two texts on pages 108–110. Then answer these questions.**

1. What type of texts are they?

2. What is the topic of each text?

D. **Choose one text to read. Take one minute to skim it. Then answer the questions below without looking back at the article.**

1. What is the text about?

2. Imagine you are writing a paper on the history of extreme skiing. Will you find some of the information you need in this text?

3. Imagine you are writing a paper on physically challenged people. Will you find some of the information you need in this text?

4. What are two things you learned by skimming?

E. **Now read the article you chose. As you read, check your answers to the questions in part D, above.**

Kristen Ulmer loves extreme sports. This biographical article describes her life as a risk taker and a thrill seeker.

Catching
BIG AIR

Kristen Ulmer takes risks for a living. When she skis she "goes big" all the time, doing big jumps and "catching big air."[1] She throws her 5-foot-8-inch, 135-pound
5 body off 70-foot cliffs. She skis 50-degree mountain slopes in Alaska.

She is the only woman to have skied down Wyoming's Grand Teton, one of the steepest slopes in the United States.
10 She loves extreme sports so much that she is also an ice climber, a paraglider, and a downhill mountain biker.

Extreme sports have helped Ulmer gain the self-confidence she didn't have
15 as a child. In elementary school in New Hampshire she didn't have many friends. "I didn't seem to fit in. I was alone a lot." Skiing, which she started at age seven, became a way to express
20 herself. She skied a lot through her teens, joining the U.S. Freestyle Ski Team in 1985.

Ulmer's great competence led her to become one of the first skiers to
25 participate in a new sport: extreme skiing—doing stunts[2] while skiing down extremely steep, difficult slopes. When she left the U.S. ski team in 1992, she entered the first extreme skiing
30 championships and won the women's division. After that experience, Ulmer became a professional extreme skier. At 34, she was called the original goddess of extreme and the best female
35 extreme skier in the world. In *Powder* magazine's 2001 list of the 50 best skiers in North America, Ulmer was the only woman in the top 10.

Ulmer is an example of the ultimate[3]
40 risk taker. However, taking risks often results in injuries. At one point in her career, Ulmer had knee surgery five times in four years and was in rehab[4] constantly. "The more time you spend
45 taking risks, the more chances you have of getting hurt or killed," says Ulmer. "Some of that risk is in my control, some isn't. But nothing I do is careless. You don't get to where I
50 am by going out and catching 50-foot air the first time. I did hundreds of 1-foot jumps before I ever did a 50-foot jump."

Sometimes, however, things do
55 get out of control. Ulmer's scariest moment was surviving a series of

[1] **catching big air:** a term used in skiing to describe a very high jump
[2] **stunt:** a very dangerous action that shows great strength and skill
[3] **ultimate:** the greatest or best
[4] **rehab:** abbreviation for rehabilitation, the process of working to bring the body back to good condition

100- to 200-mph avalanches.[5] She was skiing with three other people on a 55-degree slope in the mountains near 60 Chamonix, France. Helicopter rescuers, expecting to find four bodies, found the skiers alive, clinging to the side of the mountain.

After that experience, Ulmer says she 65 has become a little more careful. She's also trying to do new things. In addition to extreme skiing, she gives speeches to young people and business executives. She doesn't suggest that they take risks, 70 but she says, "I tell them to go big. That's a reference to doing a big jump and catching big air while skiing, but it applies to everyday life, too. I talk about the importance of going big in whatever 75 you do. Don't do it halfway."

Adapted from *USA Today*

[5] **avalanche:** a large amount of snow that suddenly moves down a mountain

13 READ B

This biographical article tells the story of Mark Wellman, a man willing to risk life and limb for the excitement and challenge of extreme sports.

Mark Wellman

Mark Wellman is a skier, a rock climber, and a kayaker. This description doesn't make him seem very different from other 5 athletes, but he is. He does all these sports without the use of his legs. Wellman has been in a wheelchair for more than 20 10 years, since he was 22 years old.

In 1982, while climbing a high peak in California, Mark 15 took a 100-foot fall. "I don't remember much about the night I spent alone near Seven Gables Peak," 20 says Wellman. "I was hungry and cold and I had no feeling in my legs." After his fall, Mark was in the hospital for seven months.

When Mark became a 25 paraplegic,[1] he felt sorry for himself for quite a while. Then one day he saw a picture of a man in a wheelchair 30 going up a mountain, hanging from climbing ropes. The picture made Mark want to climb again, 35 and he knew he could find a way to do it. While working as a park ranger in

[1] **paraplegic:** someone who is unable to move the lower part of the body

Yosemite National Park, Mark
40 met rock climber Michael Corbett.
Soon after they met, Mark and
Michael decided to scale[2] every
climber's dream: Yosemite's
magnificent El Capitan. Together,
45 Mark and Michael designed the
clothing and equipment Mark
needed to complete one of the
most difficult climbs in North
America. To train himself, Mark
50 swam, lifted weights, and
practiced climbing for months.

On the morning of July 19,
1989, Michael Corbett and Mark
Wellman began the climb. It was
55 a slow and difficult process.
Corbett's job was to move ahead of
Wellman and anchor[3] the ropes
that Mark used to pull himself up.
Once Mark raised himself a
60 certain distance, Michael would
climb back down. Then he would
carry their 200 pounds of gear up
to the spot where Mark was
waiting. At times the temperatures
65 rose to 105 degrees. Some days,
strong winds blew the two
climbers ten feet from the edge of
the cliff. After seven days of
incredibly hard work, Mark and
70 Michael completed the 3,569-foot

vertical climb. Mark said it was
like doing 7,000 pull-ups.[4] By
reaching the top, Mark became
the first rock climber to use only
75 his arms to scale El Capitan.

Mark and Michael's shared
desire to climb El Capitan, their
long months of preparation, and
the actual event, resulted in a
80 strong friendship between the
men. Together they found a way
to make Mark's dream come true.
After the climb many people were
greatly moved[5] by Mark's strong
85 desire to reach his goal and by
Michael's commitment to help
his friend.

Some people may think that
Mark Wellman has had enough
90 adventure in his life, but he
doesn't agree. He still loves the
outdoors as well as the risks and
challenges of extreme sports.
He continues to take risks despite
95 his physical condition. He even
climbed El Capitan again in 1999.
Mark doesn't consider himself
disabled because he can
accomplish almost anything he
100 wants to. "My whole thing," says
Wellman, "is finding another way."

[2] **scale:** to climb up something high
[3] **anchor:** to attach something and hold it in place so it cannot move
[4] **pull-ups:** a type of exercise that strengthens the arms
[5] **moved:** filled with emotion

14 SHARE WHAT YOU LEARNED

A. Work with a partner who read the same text.

1. Read the focus questions for your text in the chart below.

2. Discuss the questions and write the answers.

FOCUS QUESTIONS FOR TEXT A
1. How is Kristen Ulmer different from most other athletes?
2. What kinds of risks has she taken? What kind of injuries did she get?
3. Describe Ulmer's scariest experience.
4. What advice does Ulmer give other people about how to live life? Why?

FOCUS QUESTIONS FOR TEXT B
1. How is Mark Wellman different from most other athletes?
2. How did he get injured? What kind of injuries did he get?
3. What was Mark's dream? How did he prepare for it?
4. Why did Mark and Michael become such good friends?

B. With your partner, find a pair who read a different text and form a team.

1. Share the topic of your text with your teammates.

2. Take turns sharing the answers to the focus questions.

3. Add any other information from the text you remember.

15 SHARE WHAT YOU THINK

Discuss these questions with your teammates. Then share your answers with the class.

1. How are Mark Wellman and Kristen Ulmer similar? How are they different?

2. Why do you think they take life-threatening risks?

3. What did they learn from doing extreme sports?

4. What risks should people take? What risks shouldn't they take? Why?

16 REFLECT ON WHAT YOU READ IN THIS UNIT

Interview

Read the questions and think about your answers. Then interview a partner. With your partner, discuss what people can learn from taking risks.

1. What challenges do you have in your life? What do you do in these difficult situations?

2. What are some risks that you've taken in your life? What happened?

Chart and Write

A. While many people enjoy extreme sports, others believe extreme sports should not be allowed. Work with a small group to discuss how the ideas in the chart support each side of the argument. Then, add some ideas of your own.

For Extreme Sports	Against Extreme Sports
People experience challenges.	Children may think these sports are easy and want to try them.
Extreme sports emphasize individual excellence.	Extreme sports are usually expensive.

B. Write a paragraph stating whether you are for or against extreme sports. Use the information from the chart to support your opinion.

Research

Read more about extreme sports.

1. Using the Internet or an encyclopedia, look up *extreme sports*, *surfing*, *skydiving*, or *skateboarding*.

2. Read and take notes on one or more sections of an article you find.

3. Bring your notes to class and report on the information you found.

Unit 8

Staying in Touch

In this unit you will:

● read about telecommunications in the U.S.
● learn to identify patterns of organization in a paragraph

WHAT DO YOU KNOW ABOUT TELECOMMUNICATIONS?

A. Look at the cartoon. What is the cartoonist's message? Do you agree or disagree? Discuss your ideas with your classmates.

B. Think about these questions. Discuss your answers with a partner. Then share your ideas with your classmates.

1. Which invention changed communications more, the telegraph or the telephone? Why?

2. Which invention was more important to society, the Internet or the cell phone? Why?

3. What does *progress* mean to you? Does it include advances in technology? Why or why not?

A. Take the quiz. Mark the statements true (T) or false (F). Check your answers after you read the article on pages 116–117.

Telecommunications: A History Quiz

____ **1.** The United States was the birthplace of electronic communications.

____ **2.** In 1830 people communicated by telegraph.

____ **3.** Samuel Morse was the inventor of the telegraph.

____ **4.** Telegraphs were easy to use and most people had them at home.

____ **5.** The inventor of the telephone was born in Scotland.

____ **6.** The United States sent up the first communications satellite.

____ **7.** Scientists invented e-mail and the Internet at the same time.

____ **8.** Businesspeople were the first to use mobile phones in their cars.

B. Work in a small group. Read these sentences about a new computer security program. Guess which word or phrase has a meaning similar to the underlined word in each sentence. Check your guesses after you read the article on pages 116–117.

1. Our latest <u>invention</u> is ready: a new computer security program!

    a. creation   b. person   c. idea

2. With this program, the information on your computer is private. No one can <u>access</u> your files.

    a. lose and find   b. see and use   c. stop and start

3. Our security program is in a special language. Not everyone can <u>decode</u> it.

    a. hear   b. read   c. speak

4. <u>Contact</u> us by phone or e-mail to order your program.

    a. communicate with   b. hear from   c. send to

5. Once you place your order, you will <u>receive</u> a copy of the program in two days, free!

    a. send   b. read   c. get

6. If you are not <u>satisfied</u>, send the security program back and we will refund your money. Your satisfaction is guaranteed!

    a. sure   b. ready   c. happy

Authors use specific patterns to organize the information in texts. These **patterns of organization** show the relationships among ideas. Recognizing these patterns will help you understand and remember what you read.

Two common patterns of organization are:

1. **list:** a series of supporting details that add new thoughts
2. **sequence:** a series of supporting details in chronological order (time order). Sequences often include dates or times.

To identify the pattern, look for specific words or phrases, called **transitions**.

Pattern	Transitions
List	as, also, another, in addition, one more
Sequence	before, after, first, second, next, now, then, later, finally, during, while

Practice Identifying Patterns of Organization

A. **Read the paragraphs below and identify the pattern of organization for each one. Then underline the transition words that helped you decide.**

> In the 1870s, Alexander Graham Bell and Elisha Gray were busy inventing the telephone, separately! Before Bell completed his work, Elisha Gray invented a receiver, but he could not make a successful transmitter. Only after Bell designed a transmitter, could Gray complete his own telephone. On February 14, 1876, both men went to the U.S. patent office to register their inventions. Because Bell arrived two hours before Gray did, Alexander Graham Bell, and not Elisha Gray, is known as the inventor of the telephone.

1. The pattern of organization is a (list/sequence).

> Voice mail, e-mail, and the Internet are valuable tools for any business. They allow a company to communicate with customers quickly anywhere in the world. In addition, they make it easy for new and old customers to contact the company and buy more products. The use of telecommunications also enables employees to contact each other in order to solve problems efficiently. A strong telecommunications system is part of every successful company's story.

2. The pattern of organization is a (list/sequence).

B. **Work with a partner. Highlight the ideas from each paragraph that the author presents in a list or sequence.**

Use Your Reading Skills

A. Preview the article below and answer these questions.

1. What is the topic of the article?

2. What do you already know about the topic?

3. What do you predict you will learn in the article?

B. Scan the first paragraph to identify the pattern of organization (list or sequence). Underline the transition words you find.

3 READ

The United States measures more than 3000 miles east to west and 1,700 miles north to south. It's not surprising that a country of this size would be the birthplace of telecommunications: the science of communicating over great distances. This textbook article gives a brief history of telecommunications in the U.S.

Telecommunications in the United States—From Dot to Dash!

Before the middle of the 19th century, people in the United States contacted each other by mail, but the mail delivery was terribly slow. In those days it took six months for a letter to go from Washington D.C. to California. That changed in 1844 when Samuel Morse
5 invented the telegraph. After that, faster long-distance communication was possible, but it still wasn't easy. Telegraph messages were sent in Morse code—a system of dots and dashes that represented the letters of the alphabet. Only trained operators[1] could send, receive, and decode, or read, these messages. Then after a message was decoded, a messenger had to deliver it.
10 It took many years to put up telegraph lines, the wires that connected all the telegraph offices in the country. In the meantime, sending a telegram from coast to coast took at least 24 days. For example, in 1849, a telegram from New York to California would go first to a telegraph office in St. Joseph, Missouri. (That was as far west as the telegraph lines reached.) Then it went
15 by stagecoach[2] the remaining 2,300 miles. Twenty-four days was better than six months, but it was still too long.

By 1861, telegraph lines stretched from coast to coast. Soon after, engineers laid a cable[3] on the floor of the Atlantic Ocean, making it possible to send telegrams to Europe. Finally, people could send written messages
20 across the country and across the sea in seconds, but they still weren't satisfied; they wanted to be able to talk to one another.

Telecommunications took a giant step forward in 1876 when a Scottish immigrant, Alexander Graham Bell, patented[4] the first telephone in Boston. Unlike a telegraph, anyone could use a phone and communicate by voice

[1] **operator:** someone who runs a communication system such as a telegraph or telephone system
[2] **stagecoach:** a vehicle pulled by horses, used as a form of transportation in the past
[3] **cable:** a group of wires that carry an electronic signal across land or under water
[4] **patent:** to apply to the government for the rights to exclusively make or sell an invention

25 rather than mechanical clicks. The telephone had great advantages for many people. First of all, businesspeople could communicate directly with their clients. There was no need to go through an operator. Second, newspaper reporters were able to phone in their stories quickly, so news traveled faster. In addition, families throughout the country could stay in touch. It's no
30 wonder that telephone lines soon replaced telegraph lines, and telephone calls took the place of telegraph messages.

In 1957 the Russians sent the first man-made satellite,[5] Sputnik, into space, and the world of telecommunications changed again. Soon after, space satellites could transmit, or send, telephone signals to just about anywhere in the world.
35 This marked the beginning of global telecommunications. Talking to people across the globe became as easy as telephoning someone across the street.

In 1969, using satellite communications and telephone lines, U.S. government scientists in the Advanced Research Project Agency (ARPA) started a telecommunications revolution. By linking, or connecting,
40 computers, the scientists created the ARPANET. This system allowed researchers at one university to access, or see and use, information from computers at other universities. They also used the system to share research results and ideas. ARPANET was the start of the Internet. Using ARPANET, scientists also found a way to send written messages from one
45 computer to another, thus inventing electronic mail (e-mail) in 1971. When the general public started using the Internet, e-mail became an important means of communication. Not only was e-mail faster than traditional mail, but it also made it possible to communicate with hundreds of people at the same time.
50 The invention of a phone that didn't use telephone lines marked the next stage of telecommunications: mobile[6] communication. Police officers first used mobile phones in their patrol cars. Then business people began using car phones as a way to do business while they were "on the road." Later, the invention of cell phones allowed people to take their phones with them
55 wherever they went. At first, cell phones weren't very popular because they were expensive to own and operate. As the technology improved, the costs decreased. By 2004, 53 percent of Americans owned a cell phone. This percentage continues to grow, as the cost of using these phones goes down.

With all the advances in telecommunications, it's hard to imagine the six-
60 month journey of a 19th century letter. Today, e-mails move around the world, from sender to recipient, in seconds. The ease of using a cell phone helps families and friends to stay in touch and enables businesses to participate in the global economy. Twenty-first-century communication is almost instantaneous. It's fast and easy. Looking at its history, it seems very
65 likely that technology will make telecommunications even faster and easier in the years to come.

---

[5] **satellite:** a spacecraft that is sent into orbit around the earth
[6] **mobile:** moveable, portable

4 PROCESS WHAT YOU READ

A. Write your answers to the questions below. Then scan the text to check your answers.

1. In the 1800s, how long did it take for a letter to go from the East to the West?

2. When was the telegraph invented?

3. Who was the inventor?

4. When was the telephone invented?

5. Who patented the first telephone?

6. When did global communications get its start?

7. What was ARPANET?

8. What percentage of Americans owned a cell phone in 2004?

B. Think about these questions. Then discuss them with your classmates.

1. Dots and dashes were part of Morse code, but the word *dash* also means "to move quickly." Look back at the title of the article. Why do you think the author chose this title?

2. Imagine that tomorrow there will be no more telephones or computers and we will have to use the telegraph to communicate. How will life change?

3. How does progress in telecommunications affect your daily life.

5 WORK WITH THE VOCABULARY

Scan the article to find the words or phrases below. Use the context clues you find to complete the chart.

Vocabulary	Paragraph	Synonym or Definition
decode	1	read
telegraph line	2	
replaced	4	
transmit	5	
global	5	
linking	6	
access	6	
instantaneous	8	

6 GET READY TO READ ABOUT: Cell Phones

A. Work in a small group. Imagine you're preparing for a hike. You can bring only ten items with you. Look at the list below and decide which items are most important for your hike. Explain your choices to your classmates.

RECOMMENDED ITEMS FOR A SUMMER DAY HIKE

___ sweater/light jacket	___ sunscreen	___ medications
___ plastic rain poncho	___ pocket knife	___ flashlight
___ emergency blanket	___ food	___ compass
___ water bottle	___ matches	___ map
___ wool hat	___ cord/rope	___ first aid kit

B. Discuss the questions below with your classmates.

1. Imagine you can add one more item to your list. Will you bring a cell phone? Why or why not?

2. What are a few of the pros and cons (advantages and disadvantages) of having a cell phone?

3. People often use cell phones in an emergency. Give some examples of emergency situations.

C. Put a check (✓) next to the words that you know. Ask your classmates for the meanings of the words you don't know. Look up the words no one knows in a dictionary.

___ arrest (v.)   ___ hiker   ___ injured   ___ lost (adj.)

___ rescue   ___ search   ___ unprepared   ___ wilderness

Use Your Reading Skills

A. Preview the article on pages 120–121 and answer these questions.

1. What is the source of the article? Who is the author?

2. What is the topic of the article?

3. What do you already know about the topic?

4. What do you think you will learn about the topic?

B. Scan the first paragraph of the article to identify the pattern of organization.

C. Read the article quickly, skipping any words you don't know. Time your reading. Put the start time at the top and the end time at the bottom. Then answer the questions in exercise A and exercise B on page 121, section 8, exercise A.

🕐 **Start time** _____

Cell phones are an important part of 21st century telecommunications, but sometimes people use them at the wrong time or in the wrong place. This newspaper article discusses the pros and cons of using cell phones in the wilderness.

The Call in the Wild: Cell Phones Hit the Trail

The cell phone call came from Olympic National Park in Washington State. "I need a rescue," the hiker said. Park rangers[1] first asked the caller if he was lost. No, the hiker said, he knew where he was. Then they asked if he was injured. No, he wasn't hurt. Did he have enough food? Yes. Well then, they finally asked, what was the problem? "He had a meeting in Seattle," said Larry Nickey, search-and-rescue coordinator for the park. "He didn't have time to hike out."

Needless to say, the park rangers did not send in a chopper,[2] although the man offered to pay all expenses. In fact, the rangers finally told the not-lost, not-hungry, not-injured hiker that if he had a commercial helicopter service come get him, they would arrest him.

Cell phones are everywhere now, not just in cars and restaurants and on busy streets. More than half the adults in the United States use cell phones regularly, according to Gartner Inc., a technology research firm. So it's no surprise that hikers take them into the wilderness, or the woods—sometimes for safety, sometimes just to chat. For example, one hiker, after a difficult two-day climb to the top of Mount Ranier, pulled out his cell phone and called his wife. "Hi, honey, guess where I am?" he asked.

"We do have cases where the cell phone has seriously helped us," Mr. Nickey said. "In one instance, a hiker fell and broke his leg. A friend used a cell phone to call the park rangers. Rescuers hiked in and carried him out. This was a case where a cell phone actually rescued someone from harm. But every year one or two people, who just didn't bother to take a map, call in because they're lost. Those are the ones that drive us crazy," said Mr. Nickey.

Cell phones are great for emergencies. The problem that search-and-rescue workers are finding is that people define emergencies differently. To one person, it's a broken leg. To another, it's a meeting in Seattle. Furthermore, people fool themselves into thinking that cell phones provide more safety than they do. One of the most obvious problems with cell phones, either in the mountains of Olympic National Park or on the West Side Highway in Manhattan, is that they often don't work.

[1] **park ranger:** a person who takes care of the animals, plants, and people in a public park
[2] **chopper:** helicopter

Cell phones should never take the place of proper preparation for hiking and backpacking (or for taking a car trip, for that matter). Colonel Ron Alie is in charge of the New Hampshire Fish and Game Department's Search-and-Rescue Department. He doesn't understand why people bring cell phones into the wild. "After all," he says, "they don't tell you where you are. You can't eat them, and you can't drink them. And they don't provide you with any shelter."

The New Hampshire Department of Fish and Game has a website with a page that lists the 31 items required for a summer day hike. (A cell phone is not on that list.) Hikers who don't read the list and go unprepared into the wilderness have to pay the price if they need rescuing. "If you come out here and you don't meet our standards, we will be sending you a bill for that rescue," Colonel Alie said. However, if a hiker knows what he or she is doing and has the proper equipment, whether or not to carry a phone is completely up to that person. "Hey," Colonel Alie said, "if you want to take a TV up there with you, be my guest."

Adapted from an article by James Gorman for the New York Times

 **End time** _____

PROCESS WHAT YOU READ

A. **Mark the answers true (T) or false (F) without looking back at the article. Then check your answers on page 135. Follow the instructions for recording your comprehension score and reading speed on the inside back cover.**

____ 1. A man once used his cell phone to ask for a helicopter rescue.

____ 2. Some hikers are packing cell phones instead of maps.

____ 3. Emergency means different things to different people.

____ 4. It's against the law to bring a cell phone into a national park.

____ 5. Search-and-rescue workers will always help you, free of charge.

B. **Choose the sentence that best states the main idea of the article.**

1. Cell phones are good in emergencies, but not everybody has the same idea about what an emergency is.

2. Many people are using cell phones to call for a rescue when they're lost in the wilderness.

3. Cell phones are good for emergencies in the wilderness, but they're no substitute for preparation.

C. **Work with a partner. Review the fourth paragraph of the article. Then write a two-sentence summary of it. Share your summary with your classmates.**

9 WORK WITH THE VOCABULARY

A. Use these words to complete the news story below.

a. after	b. finally	c. for	d. hiker	e. lost
f. rescue	g. search	h. then	i. uninjured	j. unprepared

Cell Phone Rescues Woman Lost in Mountains for 3 Days

Last week, Tim Lange lost his cell phone when he was hiking in the mountains of Sky Park. He tried to look for the phone, but it got too dark to see so he had to go home.

That same week, another ____, Jean McMullin, got ____ in the mountains. Park officials tried to ____ for McMullin, but bad weather made it difficult.

____ 72 hours, the park office received a phone call—from Jean McMullin! She told officials her location and they were able to ____

her. She was hungry and cold, but ____. Later, McMullin explained, "I found the phone in some bushes near a tree. ____ two days the phone didn't work, but ____ on day three, it ____ worked."

A park official told reporters, "So many people are coming into the mountains ____ these days. Maybe we should put cell phones under every tree."

A grateful Jean McMullin returned the phone to Tim Lange the next day.

B. Match the phrases with the words or phrases that have a similar meaning. Look back at the article on pages 120–121 to check your answers. Then, with a partner, write a new sentence using each phrase.

____ 1. pay a price

____ 2. needless to say

____ 3. drive someone crazy

____ 4. be my guest

a. obviously

b. make someone upset

c. go ahead and do what you want

d. be punished, suffer for doing something

C. Scan the article on pages 120–121 to find these words. Highlight the context clues for each one.

a. injured   b. wilderness   c. chat

A. In a small group, decide which communication tool is better for each situation below. List two reasons to support each decision. Then explain your decisions to your classmates.

For This Situation	Is It Better to Phone or Email?		Why?
	Phone	E-mail	
Asking for help on homework			
Thanking someone for a gift			
Giving bad news			
Inviting someone to a party			
Sharing information at work			
Saying "hi" to a friend you haven't seen for years			

B. Put a check (✓) next to the words you know. Ask your classmates for the meanings of the words you don't know. Look up the words no one knows in a dictionary.

___ boon   ___ conveniently   ___ establish   ___ evolution

___ impact (n.)   ___ portable   ___ resist   ___ simultaneously

C. Preview the texts on pages 124–126. Then answer these questions.

1. What is the topic of each text?

2. What do you already know about the topics?

D. Choose one text to read. Skim the first paragraph and answer these questions.

1. What is the main idea of the first paragraph?

2. What do you predict you will learn in the text?

E. Preview the focus questions for your text on page 127. Identify which questions ask for a list of information and which questions ask for a date or a sequence of events. Highlight the answers to the questions as you read the text.

This web page gives a brief history of the telephone and shows its evolution from a simple invention to a complex communication tool.

File   Edit   View   Tools   Help

◄   ►   ⊗   ⇄   🏠
Back   Forward   Stop   Refresh   Home

The Telephone

"Mr. Watson, come here. I want you." Alexander Graham Bell spoke these seven ordinary words to his assistant, Thomas Watson. These words become extraordinary, however, when you realize that they were the first words Bell spoke over his new invention: the telephone. On that day, March 10, 1876, the first
5   "emergency call" occurred when Bell spilled some acid[1] on his clothing and Watson heard his call for help through the wires of the new invention. On that day, neither man had any idea of the impact this invention would have on the United States and the world.

At first, Bell didn't plan to invent the telephone. He was trying to develop a
10 telegraph that could send several messages over the same wire simultaneously. As he worked, he discovered that a wire could transmit sound, and the idea for the telephone was born. Shortly after that, Bell built and patented[2] the first telephone.

Telephones soon started to appear everywhere. By the 1890s, many Americans had telephones at home. Later, coin-operated pay telephones were put in public
15 places. Once the telephone linked cities, it wasn't long before it also linked countries. In 1955 a transatlantic cable allowed North Americans to talk to people in Europe. Then, in the 1960s, communications satellites enabled people to talk to others almost anywhere in the world.

Mobile, or portable, phones marked the next step in the telephone's evolution.
20 They first appeared in the 1920s in New York City police cars. Even though these phones were portable, they were too big and only worked in small areas, so the public wasn't interested. In 1978 the invention of the cell phone, small enough to fit in a pocket or purse, changed public opinion. By 1981, cell phones were used throughout the country. Today, children use cell phones to stay in touch with their
25 parents; business people use cell phones to contact their offices and clients; and most importantly, drivers and others use cell phones to make emergency calls, sometimes saving a life. In fact, scientists at Bell Labs in New Jersey have made a small change in cell phone design that will save even more lives. Their new phone

[1] **acid:** a chemical that can burn through clothing and skin
[2] **patent:** to apply to the government for the exclusive rights to make and sell an invention

can monitor, or check, a person's pulse[3] and breathing rate, even when the phone is
30 turned off. Emergency workers will be able to use the signal from a cell phone to
locate people and then assist, or help, them during earthquakes or other disasters.

As with any invention, the telephone has created some problems. Phone calls
often interrupt time with family and friends. Telemarketers make unwanted calls to
people at home, hoping to convince them to buy their products. The portability of
35 cell phones has created another problem: Many people expect their co-workers or
employees to be available at any time, no matter where they are. This makes it
hard to enjoy time away from work. One other problem is that people use cell
phones while simultaneously doing other things, such as driving. This can be very
dangerous. For the most part, however, the telephone has been a boon to a country
40 with over 290 million people. It has allowed families to stay in touch despite the
separation of many miles; it has helped businesses reach more customers; it has
saved millions of lives with emergency calls to police, fire fighters, and paramedics;
and it has enabled people to reach out to each other, friend to friend, and say,
"Come here. I need you."

[3] **pulse:** the regular beat in the body as the heart pumps blood through it

12 READ B

*This web page talks about the evolution of e-mail from a means of communication for scientists
to an important communication tool for the general public.*

File   Edit   View   Tools   Help   _ □ ×

◄   ►   ⊗   ⇄   🏠
Back   Forward   Stop   Refresh   Home

MODERN MAIL

Imagine looking at your computer screen and reading
"QWERTYUIOP." Not much to get excited about, is it? Yet in
1971, this message was very exciting. When Ray Tomlinson, a
scientist working for the Advanced Research Projects Agency
5 (ARPA) sent this ten-letter message from his computer to his
co-worker's computer, e-mail (electronic mail) was born. That first message didn't
say much—it was just the first ten letters on the computer keyboard—but the
impact on world telecommunications and on American culture was great.

✉

More than 50 percent of people in the United States use e-mail. This technology
10 has brought dramatic changes to the way people communicate. Messages can be
transmitted in seconds. In the past, it took a lot of time to write and send a formal
letter. Now, the speed and informality of e-mail make it acceptable for written
messages to be short and to the point. Friends and co-workers often use everyday

language and abbreviations or symbols such as "u" for "you" "BTW" for "by the
15 way" or ";-") for "just joking." (Although, this type of language is generally not
used in e-mails about business or other important matters.)

E-mail allows direct communication, and many Americans are taking advantage of
this. For example, employees are e-mailing ideas for new products to the company
CEO[1] and getting a personal reply. Citizens can contact the president, members of
20 Congress, or local government officials[2] in seconds. Because the process is so easy,
there has been a great increase in activism—people are expressing their opinions and
making suggestions for social change.

Another line of communication has opened through e-mail: the line between
generations. From homes all across America comes a steady clicking—the sound of
25 parents at the computer, typing messages to their college-age sons and daughters;
grandparents e-mailing their grandchildren; or people writing to long-lost relatives.
In the United States it is no longer common for grandparents, parents, and children
all to live together. Nevertheless, the extended family is alive and well, connected
through e-mail.

30 At one time, it was necessary to make most social connections in person. Now,
thanks to e-mail, first-time, informal conversations can take place on-line. Shy
people, who find it hard to talk face-to-face, often prefer e-mail. At their computers
they feel free to share the feelings they would never express in person.

The speed and convenience of e-mail can sometimes be a problem, though.
35 Advertisers are able to send thousands of ads (spam) out with a single click. The
single click also can be a problem for the average e-mail user. People often don't
realize that they've accidentally sent a private message to a long list of people until
it's too late. In addition, unlike a regular conversation, where a quick apology can
usually erase an angry remark, angry e-mails stay around for a long time. E-mail
40 messages often remain on a computer's hard drive even after they're deleted, so
writers need to think carefully before they click "send."

For most people, however, the advantages of e-mail outnumber the disadvantages.
This evolution in communication has become a part of many Americans' daily lives.
It has helped people establish or re-establish relationships, connect with a wide
45 range of people, and quickly and conveniently get their ideas across. And it all
began with just ten letters, "QWERTYUIOP."

[1] **CEO:** chief executive officer, the top job in a company
[2] **official:** someone in a responsible position who makes important decisions

13 SHARE WHAT YOU LEARNED

A. Work with a partner who read the same text.

   1. Read the focus questions for your text in the chart below.

   2. Discuss the questions and write the answers.

FOCUS QUESTIONS FOR TEXT A
1. When was the phone invented and by whom?
2. What is the story of the first telephone call?
3. How has the use of telephones changed from the time of their invention to the present?
4. What problems has the telephone created?

FOCUS QUESTIONS FOR TEXT B
1. When was e-mail invented and by whom?
2. What is the story of the first e-mail message?
3. What are the advantages of using e-mail to communicate?
4. What are some of the problems that can happen with e-mail?

B. With your partner, find a pair who read a different text and form a team.

   1. Share the topic of your text with your teammates.

   2. Take turns sharing the answers to the focus questions.

   3. Add any other information from the text you remember.

14 SHARE WHAT YOU THINK

Discuss these questions with your teammates. Then share your answers with the class.

1. Video phones allow people to see each other when they're on the phone. Do you think this is a good addition to Bell's invention? Why or why not?

2. Do you think people will use e-mail differently in the future? Why or why not?

3. The telephone and e-mail allow people from all over the world to communicate with each other. Do differences in culture affect their communication? Why or why not?

4. Do you think the advantages of using the telephone or e-mail outweigh the problems? Why? How do you avoid or deal with the problems?

15 REFLECT ON WHAT YOU READ

Interview

Read the questions and think about your answers. Then, interview a partner.
With your partner, decide if the percentages are different for people living outside
the U.S.

What percentage of your time do you spend . . .

a. writing letters or postcards?   c. talking on the phone?
b. writing e-mails?   d. talking face-to-face?

Chart and Write

A. Think about the telephone and e-mail. Write a list of characteristics that describes
each way of communicating. Using your lists, follow the model to create a Venn
diagram. Put items that are common to both ways of communicating in the
"Both" section.

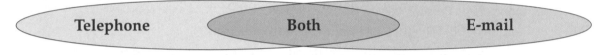

B. Using the information in the chart, write a paragraph that compares and contrasts
the ways of communicating. Share your paragraph with a partner.

16 REFLECT ON YOUR READING STRATEGIES

Read the questions in the chart, and choose the answers that best describe your use
of the reading strategies. Then with your classmates, discuss which strategies are the
most helpful and which ones you need to practice more.

Strategy	How often do you use this strategy outside of this class?			How helpful is this strategy?		
	Always	Sometimes	Never	Very	A little	Not
Previewing and Predicting						
Scanning						
Using context clues						
Finding the main idea						
Summarizing						
Skimming						
Identifying Patterns of Organization						

Answer Key

Unit 1   The American Quilt

**WHAT DO YOU KNOW ABOUT
IMMIGRATION?** (p. 1) *(Answers vary.)*

1. GET READY TO READ ABOUT: Immigration

Exercise A and B (p. 2) *(Answers vary.)*
Exercise C (p. 2)
1. a   2. a   3. c   4. b   5. a

2. BUILDING READING SKILLS: Previewing and Predicting

Practice Previewing and Predicting (p. 3)
1. Immigration
2. immigration trends; *(Answers vary.)*
3. Eric Wolff, PhD; Population News Magazine
4. *(Answers vary.)*
5. Information about the population of the U.S. in 2050
6. *(Answers vary.)*

Use Your Reading Skills (p. 4)
1. immigrants in the U.S.
2. the history of U.S. immigration and its effect on American culture
3. population changes from 2000–2065
4. *(Answers vary.)*

4. PROCESS WHAT YOU READ

Exercise A (p. 6)
1. T   2. F   3. T   4. T
5. F   6. F   7. T   8. F

Exercise B (p. 6)
In 2000: Asian 4%, Black/African American 12%, Hispanic/Latino 13%, Native American and Hawaiian 1%, White 67%.
In 2065: Asian 10%, Black/African American 13%, Hispanic/Latino 28%, Native American and Hawaiian 1%, White 48%.
1. Asian +6%, Black/African American +1%, Hispanic/Latino +15%, Native American and Hawaiian 0%, White −19%
2. *(Answers vary.)*

Exercise C (p. 6) *(Answers vary.)*

5. WORK WITH THE VOCABULARY

Exercise A (p. 7)
1. e   2. d   3. a   4. b   5. c

Exercise B (p. 7)
1a. education   1b. educate
2a. assimilate   2b. assimilation
3a. Immigration   3b. immigrate
4a. contribute   4b. contribution
5a. population   5b. populate

6. IMPROVING READING SPEED AND COMPREHENSION: Identifying Common Words

Practice Identifying Common Words (p. 8) *(Answers vary.)*

7. GET READY TO READ ABOUT: Immigrants (p. 8)

Exercise A (p. 8)
Picture on the left: Eastern Europe; 1912
Picture on the right: Japan; 1919

Exercise B (p. 8) *(Answers vary.)*

Use Your Reading Skills (p. 9)
1. book review
2. the effect of diversity on American culture
3. *(Answers vary.)*

9. PROCESS WHAT YOU READ

Exercise A (p. 10)
1. b   2. f   3. a   4. d
5. h   6. c   7. e   8. g

Exercise B (p. 10) 28

10. GET READY TO READ AND SHARE

Exercise A and B (p. 11) *(Answers vary.)*
Exercise C (p. 11)
1. Guyanese immigrants help shape Schenectady; a newspaper article
2. a Vietnamese refugee's life in Chicago; a letter.

Exercise D (p. 11) *(Answers vary.)*

13. SHARE WHAT YOU LEARNED

Focus Questions for Text A (p. 15)
1. to open his own business
2. bought homes and opened small businesses
3. Guyanese people are moving in, fixing up old homes and businesses, and working hard to develop the area.
4. *(Answers vary.)*

Focus Questions for Text B (p. 15)
1. He's a Vietnamese refugee. He needed to leave Vietnam.
2. They opened a community center, organized a neighborhood watch system, and convinced a few landlords to rent their stores to refugees at low cost.
3. It's a safe and interesting part of the city. It has many stores and restaurants.
4. *(Answers vary.)*

14. SHARE WHAT YOU THINK
(p. 15) *(Answers vary.)*

15. REFLECT ON WHAT YOU READ IN THIS UNIT (p. 16) *(Answers vary.)*

Unit 2   Getting Along

HOW DOES DIVERSITY AFFECT YOU? (p. 17) *(Answers vary.)*

1. GET READY TO READ ABOUT: Diversity

Exercise A and B (p. 18) *(Answers vary.)*
Exercise C (p. 18)
1. high   2. positive   3. know
4. aren't   5. stop   6. isn't

2. BUILDING READING SKILLS: Previewing Comprehension Questions

Practice Previewing Comprehension Questions
Exercise A (p. 19)
1. differences among people help create a more interesting environment
2. prejudice
3. organizations such as Stop the Hate offer information and programs about how to prevent prejudice
4. help students speak out against prejudice on campus

Exercise B (p. 19)
the values and traditions of different cultures; different work styles; communication skills

Use Your Reading Skills
Exercise A (p. 20)
1. diversity in the U.S.
2. *(Answers vary.)*

Exercise B (p. 20)
(See answers for Exercise A, p. 22)

4. PROCESS WHAT YOU READ

Exercise A (p. 22)
1. it is the many ways people differ from each other
2. gender, age, ethnic background, race, marital status, religion, physical ability, mental ability, language skills, life experience, etc.
3. it makes a society richer and more interesting
4. prejudice and discrimination
5. it makes laws against discrimination such as the Civil Rights Act of 1964 or Title IX of the Education Amendments of 1972
6. the history and traditions of various cultures in relation to their own
7. that two-thirds of the participants said it's important to prepare students to live in a diverse society
8. to create a workplace where everyone understands, respects, and values the differences of others

Exercise B (p. 22)
1. b   2. a   3. c   4. b

Exercise C (p. 22) *(Answers vary.)*

5. WORK WITH THE VOCABULARY

Exercise A (p. 23)
1. differences   3. different
2. differ   4. differently

Exercise B (p. 23)
create; discuss; participate; prevent;
discriminate; protect

Exercise C (p. 23)
1. create   4. discriminate
2. prevent   5. participate
3. protect   6. discuss

Exercise D (p. 23)
1. problem   3. diversity
2. dislike   4. forget

6. GET READY TO READ ABOUT:
   One View of Diversity

Exercise A (p. 24) *(Answers vary.)*

Exercise B (p. 24)
1. write a page tonight
2. because it comes out of you
3. you, true
4. *(Answers vary.)*

Use Your Reading Skills

Exercise A (p. 24)
1. Langston Hughes; *(Answers vary.)*
2. Hughes' life; *(Answers vary.)*
3. *(Answers vary.)*

Exercise B (p. 24)
(See answers for Exercise A, p. 26)

8. PROCESS WHAT YOU READ

Exercise A (p. 26)
1. no
2. in Winston-Salem; in Winston-Salem,
   then Durham, then New York City
3. by going down the steps into Harlem
   and through a park, then he crosses St.
   Nicholas, Eighth, and Seventh
   Avenues
4. the Y
5. eat, sleep, drink, be in love, work,
   read, learn, and understand life

Exercise B (p. 26)
5, 3, 6, 2, 1, 4

Exercise C (p. 26) *(Answers vary.)*

Exercise D (p. 26)
1. c   2. b   3. d   4. a

9. GET READY TO READ AND
   SHARE

Exercise A (p. 27)
1. fact   4. stereotype
2. stereotype   5. stereotype
3. fact

Exercise B and C (p. 27) *(Answers vary.)*

Exercise D (p. 27)
1. stereotypes of Native Americans
2. gaining friendship and understanding
   through song

Exercise E (p. 27) *(Answers vary.)*

12. SHARE WHAT YOU LEARNED

Focus Questions for Text A (p. 31)
1. to celebrate the strength and courage
   of the Native American people
2. because they believe it encourages
   stereotyping and discrimination
3. to keep the name but change the
   mascot; *(Answers vary.)*
4. *(Answers vary.)*

Focus Questions for Text B (p. 31)
1. to bring people together from two
   different backgrounds who shared a
   common interest and to improve
   relations between African Americans
   and Jewish Americans
2. because both African Americans and
   Jewish people have ancestors who
   were slaves
3. learning unfamiliar music and
   learning their parts in different ways
4. *(Answers vary.)*

13. SHARE WHAT YOU THINK
   (p. 31) *(Answers vary.)*

14. REFLECT ON WHAT YOU READ
   IN THIS UNIT
   (p. 32) *(Answers vary.)*

Unit 3   Looking at Looks

HOW IMPORTANT IS APPEARANCE?
(p. 33) *(Answers vary.)*

1. GET READY TO READ ABOUT:
   Body Image

Exercise A (p. 34) *(Answers vary.)*

Exercise B (p. 34)
1. happy
2. unhappiness
3. This medical treatment can change the
   shape of the face or body.
4. how someone feels about himself or
   herself
5. make people believe
6. people spend too much time thinking
   about their appearance
7. form an opinion
8. good or bad qualities

2. BUILDING READING SKILLS:
   Scanning

Practice Scanning (p. 35)
1. ⓁIndsay Ⓐllison, Ⓜ.Ⓓ.
2. ⊙Surgery of the Face, Eyes, Nose and
   Ears ⊙Wrinkle Removal ⊙Tatoo
   Removal
3. www.yearsyounger.com
4. allison@yearsyounger.com
5. ⑳Use my creams and lotions. Your
   skin will get the important vitamins it
   needs: A, B, D, E, and K.⑳
6. 504–555–1112

Use Your Reading Skills

Exercise A (p. 36)
1. the importance of personal
   appearance in the U.S.
2. *(Answers vary.)*

Exercise B (p. 36)
1. "Family Circle"   4. 23%
2. 432   5. Dr. David Sarwer
3. 13%   6. 7%

4. PROCESS WHAT YOU READ

Exercise A (p. 38)
1. it plays a big role in Americans' focus
   on image; ads try to convince people
   to do something to improve their looks
2. because they are dissatisfied with
   their looks and hope that surgery will
   help them feel better about themselves
3. 55% of first impressions are based on
   appearance, 38% on body language,
   and 7% on what you say
4. because they have a desire to feel better
   about themselves, make a positive
   impression, and succeed

Exercise B (p. 38)
1. a.   2. b   3.c

Exercise C (p. 38) *(Answers vary.)*

5. Work with the Vocabulary (p. 38)
1. e   2. a   3. c   4. f   5. d   6. b

6. IMPROVING READING SPEED
   AND COMPREHENSION: Skipping
   Words You Don't Know

Practice Skipping Words You Don't
Know

Exercise A (p. 39)
1. c   2. b   3. a

Exercise B (p. 39) *(Answers vary.)*

7. GET READY TO READ ABOUT:
   Business Dressing (p. 39)
   (Answers vary.)

Use Your Reading Skills

Exercise A (p. 40)
1. business clothing
2. *(Answers vary.)*

Exercise B (p. 40) *(See answers for Exercise
A and Exercise B, p. 42)*

9. PROCESS WHAT YOU READ

Exercise A (p. 42)
1. F   2. T   3. T   4. F   5. T

Exercise B (p. 42)
1. 50 percent
2. IBM; Morgan Stanley
3. "Americans will wear a combination
   of formal business and dressier casual
   clothes."

10. WORK WITH THE VOCABULARY (p. 42)

1a. comfortably 1b. comfortable
2a. productive 2b. productively
3a. appropriately 3b. Appropriate
4a. conservative 4b. conservatively
5a. formal 5b. formally

11. GET READY TO READ AND SHARE

Exercise A and B (p. 43) *(Answers vary.)*
Exercise C (p. 43)
1. body art; for
2. risks of body art; against
Exercise D (p. 43) *(Answers vary.)*

14. SHARE WHAT YOU LEARNED

Focus Questions for Text A (p. 47)
1. 60% of women and 42% of men had piercings, and 20% had tattoos
2. express themselves, shock people, be in fashion, be cool, look like their favorite movie or TV stars, and because they love body art
3. color their hair, wear makeup, put on clothes, have cosmetic surgery, etc.
4. to attract a romantic partner, improve self-esteem, show membership in a group, and show independence

Focus Questions for Text B (p. 47)
1. 10% of young people had tattoos and many had piercings
2. nerve damage, cartilage damage, long healing time, infection, skin irritation, pain, diseases, allergic reactions, and skin cancer
3. get a vaccination for Hepatitis B, set limits about the number of piercings they get, find a reliable parlor or doctor who uses sterile needles, and keep tattooed and pierced areas clean
4. because they change their minds or they no longer want to have an ex-boyfriend's/girlfriends name on their bodies

15. SHARE WHAT YOU THINK (p. 47)
(Answers vary.)

16. REFLECT ON WHAT YOU READ IN THIS UNIT (p. 48) *(Answers vary.)*

Unit 4 Getting the News

How do you learn about events in the news? (p. 49) *(Answers vary.)*

1. GET READY TO READ ABOUT: News

Exercise A and B (p. 50) *(Answers vary.)*
Exercise C (p. 50)
1. the people who gather, write, and report the news
2. all the important things that happen in their community
3. Internet, computers, or cell phones
4. 24 hours a day
5. magazine, newspaper, radio, TV show
6. try to do better
7. gets the attention
8. Newspapers, radio, TV, and the Internet

2. BUILDING READING SKILLS: Using Context Clues

Practice Using Context Clues (p. 51)

circle *such as*; highlight *books, newspapers, and magazines*; example
circle *or*; highlight *got*; synonym
circle *or*; highlight *the ability to read and write*; definition
highlight *television, radio, Internet*; example
circle *not* ; highlight *just accept*; contrast

Use Your Reading Skills
Exercise A (p. 52)
1. technology and the news
2. *(Answers vary.)*
3. *(Answers vary.)*

Exercise B (p. 52)
a. killing
b. Internet, satellite and cable TV, cellular phones
c. whenever they want it
d. ask about
e. basing their stories on facts
f. focusing on the most upsetting or shocking details of a story

4. PROCESS WHAT YOU READ

Exercise A (p. 54)
1. from TV, newspapers, or radio
2. to get news on the Internet, satellite and cable TV, and cellular phones; *(Answers vary.)*
3. because they are trying to attract the same group of people; some traditional news sources are changing the way they deliver the news in order to compete and using sensationalism to attract viewers
4. from traditional sources

Exercise B (p. 54)
1. a   2. c   3. b   4. b

Exercise C (p. 54) *(Answers vary.)*

5. WORK WITH THE VOCABULARY

Exercise A (p. 55)
1. g   2. a   3. h   4. d
5. b   6. c   7. e   8. f

Exercise B (p. 55)
popular; national; information; technology; traditional; competition

Exercise C (p. 55)
1. tradition; *(Answers vary.)*
2. informational; *(Answers vary.)*
3. Competition; *(Answers vary.)*
4. popularity; *(Answers vary.)*
5. national; *(Answers vary.)*
6. technological; *(Answers vary.)*

6. GET READY TO READ ABOUT: TV News

Exercise A (p. 56) *(Answers vary.)*
Exercise B (p. 56)
1. It has the same powerful, exciting qualities as a play.
2. Brave people who do courageous things
3. are very enjoyable and hold viewers' interest
4. are very interesting
5. government issues
6. how many people watch these programs every week
7. feeling
8. exciting and dangerous experiences

Use Your Reading Skills
Exercise A (p. 56)
1. The Mediathon
2. *(Answers vary.)*
3. *(Answers vary.)*

Exercise B (p. 56)
(See answers for section 8, Exercise A, p. 58)

8. PROCESS WHAT YOU READ

Exercise A (p. 58)
1. F   2. T   3. T   4. F   5. T

Exercise B (p. 50) *(Answers vary.)*

9. WORK WITH THE VOCABULARY

Exercise A (p. 58)
a. stories of exciting adventures, brave heroes, or terrible tragedies
b. symbol
c. a lot of money
d. who knew a lot about politics and law
e. desire to know all about something
f. likes
g. entertainment
h. dropping

Exercise B (p. 58) *(Answers vary.)*

10. GET READY TO READ AND SHARE

Exercise A and B (p.59) *(Answers vary.)*
Exercise C (p. 59)
1. talk radio
2. on-line or Internet chatting
Exercise D and E (p. 59) *(Answers vary.)*

13. SHARE WHAT YOU LEARNED

Focus Questions for Text A (p. 63)
1. radio shows that feature conversation rather than music; approximately 52 million people listen to talk radio

2. because it encourages listeners to take part in the discussion and it is anonymous
3. it satisfies Americans' need to talk to each other
4. because people can listen to talk radio broadcasts on the Internet anywhere in the world

Focus Questions for Text B (p. 63)
1. exchanging information with other people over the Internet; about 37 million Americans chat on-line
2. because it's an easy way to have a social life
3. the need to connect with others and to make friends
4. stay anonymous by not giving their real names or information about where they live or work; in person, they should meet in a public place and bring friends along

14. SHARE WHAT YOU THINK (p. 63)
   (Answers vary.)

15. REFLECT ON WHAT YOU READ IN THIS UNIT (p. 64) *(Answers vary.)*

Unit 5 Feeding Body and Soul

HOW IMPORTANT IS MEALTIME IN THE U.S.? (p. 57) *(Answers vary.)*

1. GET READY TO READ ABOUT: Feeding the Soul

Exercise A and B (p. 66) *(Answers vary.)*
Exercise C (p. 66)
1. bodies
2. feed
3. makes you feel better
4. eat it slowly in order to taste all the flavors and really enjoy it
5. pleasant smells
6. big meal
7. small amount of food
8. worries

2. BUILDING READING SKILLS: Finding the Main Idea and Supporting Details
Practice Finding the Main Idea and Supporting Details
Exercise A (p. 67)
1. a. d   b. m   c. d
2. a. m   b. d   c. d
3. a. d   b. d   c. m
4. a. d   b. m   c. d

Exercise B (p. 67)
1. family meals in the U.S.
2. Many families often spend more time preparing dinner than eating it; last
3. family members spend 38 minutes preparing dinner; average family spends 26 minutes eating together;

27% of families spend less than 20 minutes at the dinner table
4. There are several popular mealtime customs; first
5. assign each person a task such as setting the table or making a dish; sharing stories; a special afternoon or evening meal on weekends

Use Your Reading Skills (p. 68)
1. benefits of sharing meals
2. food is nourishment for the body and the soul
3. last
4. memories of comforting foods include the dishes and the people who prepared them and ate them together; cooking and eating food at home strengthened relationships and showed we cared for each other

4. PROCESS WHAT YOU READ
Exercise A (p. 70)
1. Americans cooked and ate most meals at home; television, women getting into the job market, and fast food
2. many Americans are sitting down with friends and family to eat and are eating ethnic foods, farm-grown fruits and vegetables and home-cooked meals; to nourish both the body and the soul
3. it acts as a natural tranquilizer, it reduces stress and it sends messages of well-being to the brain; it's pleasurable and it can help you live a longer, healthier life
4. shopping for local, fresh food, eating with variety, and cooking at home

Exercise B (p. 70)
Paragraph 2: a   Paragraph 4: b
Paragraph 3: c   Paragraph 5: a
Exercise C (p. 70) *(Answers vary.)*

5. WORK WITH THE VOCABULARY
Exercise A (p. 71) *(Answers vary.)*
Exercise B (p. 71)
soul; memory; emotional; pleasure; supportive; healthy
Exercise C (p. 71)
1. health   4. pleasurable
2. soul   5. supportive
3. emotions   6. memorable
Exercise D (p. 71)
1. b   2. b   3. a

6. GET READY TO READ ABOUT: A Memorable Meal (p. 72)
   (Answers vary.)

Use Your Reading Skills
Exercise A (p. 72)
1. memories of eating my grandmother's home-cooked meals; my grandmother's meals

2. My grandmother took simple ingredients and, like magic, turned them into gold; the memory of my grandmother's meals nourish my soul
3. last; last
4. the meal is simple: rice, beans, meat, fried plantains, avocado and onions; my grandmother could take a few ingredients and make many combinations of dishes; the memory of my grandmother's meals reminds me of her hugs, the smells of her kitchen, the sound of laughter and the feeling of her love

8. PROCESS WHAT YOU READ (p. 74)
1. T   2. F   3. F   4. T   5. F

9. WORK WITH THE VOCABULARY (p. 74)
abuela – grandmother
chorizo – sausage
panadería – Cuban bread fresh from
bodega – Everything she needed she bought each day at the – on the corner.
tazitas of café Cubano – coffee
burrones – Cuban cookies

10. GET READY TO READ AND SHARE
Exercise A and B (p. 75) *(Answers vary.)*
Exercise C (p. 75)
1. Text A: magazine article
   Text B: brochure
2. Text A: fast food
   Text B: Slow Food USA
3. *(Answers vary.)*
Exercise D (p. 75)
Text A:
1. The Fast Growth of Fast-Food Restaurants
2. Fast-food restaurants have become a big part of American culture.
3. 3
4. fast-food restaurants are everywhere; they have changed the way people eat and the way American cities and towns look.
Text B:
1. Slow Food USA
2. Slow Food USA is an organization that supports, celebrates, and protects the food traditions of North America.
3. 1
4. Slow Food USA's goal is to rediscover the pleasure and quality in everyday life, to slow down and appreciate the traditional ways of producing, preparing, and eating food.; Slow Food supports ecological food production,

local organic farming, and regional, seasonal cooking.

Exercise E (p. 75) *(Answers vary.)*

13. SHARE WHAT YOU LEARNED

Focus Questions for Text A (p. 79)

1. Richard and Maurice McDonald decided to make food faster and sell it for less

2. many entrepreneurs from all over the country came to see the first fast-food restaurant and opened their own fast-food restaurants; fast food spread faster when Ray Kroc sold McDonald's franchises; other fast-food restaurants sold franchises, too

3. the same fast-food restaurants are all across the country so they make American cities and towns all look the same; American food is mostly the same fast food all over the country.

4. they are changing their images by building new restaurants that look like other buildings nearby and offering more diverse menus

Focus Questions for Text B (p. 79)

1. because of a fear that fast food would make all cultures the same

2. because in this age of mass production, we could easily lose these foods and the farms that produce them

3. helps people lose excess weight, maintain a normal weight, and have more satisfaction in their everyday lives

4. *(Answers vary.)*

14. SHARE WHAT YOU THINK (p. 79)

(Answers vary.)

15. REFLECT ON WHAT YOU READ IN THIS UNIT

(p. 80) *(Answers vary.)*

Unit 6   Consumer Awareness

WHAT DO YOU KNOW ABOUT CONSUMER RIGHTS? (p. 81) *(Answers vary.)*

1. GET READY TO READ ABOUT: The Consumer Movement

Exercise A (p. 82)

1. F   2. T   3. T   4. F
5. T   6. T   7. T   8. F

Exercise B (p. 82)

1. knowledge   5. strong
2. don't like   6. the way
3. good   7. must do
4. bad   8. having

2. BUILDING READING SKILLS: Summarizing a Paragraph

Practice Summarizing a Paragraph

Exercise A (p. 83)

1. Upton Sinclair wrote books about

---

some unacceptable business practices in the United States; *(Answers vary.)*

2. yes; *(Answers vary.)*

Exercise B (p. 83)

1. no; *(Answers vary.)*
2. *(Answers vary.)*
3. *(Answers vary.)*

Use Your Reading Skills

Exercise A (p. 84)

1. the consumer movement
2. *(Answers vary.)*
3. *(Answers vary.)*
4. The consumer movement has protected buyers from unfair business practices.
5. it began in the early 1900s; unfair business practices are: 1) selling unsafe products, 2) false advertising, labeling, or packaging, 3) actions that decrease competition

Exercise B (p. 84)

1890 — Sherman Act passed

early 1900s — consumer movement began

1906 — Upton Sinclair's *The Jungle*

1906 — U.S. Food and Drug Act of 1906

1914 — Federal Trade Commission began

1929 — Consumers' Research, Inc. began

1957 — Vance Packard's *The Hidden Persuaders*

1960 — Vance Packard's *The Wastemakers*

1965 — Ralph Nader's *Unsafe at Any Speed*

1966 — National Traffic and Safety Act of 1966

1970s — Consumer groups organize against high cost of products

1980s — nutritional information put on food packaging after consumers demand it

4. PROCESS WHAT YOU READ

Exercise A (p. 86)

1. because manufacturers were selling many unclean and unsafe items, so consumers wanted to control product quality

2. Upton Sinclair, Vance Packard, and Ralph Nader; Sinclair wrote *The Jungle* which described the unclean conditions in meat-packing plants and led to the U.S. Food and Drug Act of 1906. Packard wrote *The Hidden Persuaders* and *The Wastemakers* which identified some types of advertising that tried to make people buy products they didn't need. Nader wrote *Unsafe at Any Speed* which told about safety

---

problems in certain automobiles and led to the National Traffic Motor Vehicle Safety Act of 1966.

3. companies that have no competition and are able to control the supply of products and charge high prices for them; by passing the Sherman Act

4. because some ads made false claims about products

5. to have: 1) products whose quality matches their prices, 2) protection against unsafe products, 3) truthful, complete information about products of services, 4) a choice among a variety of products, 5) the right to complain about unsatisfactory products and services and get compensation when there is a good reason for a complaint

6. to follow the instructions that come with a product and use it correctly

Exercise B (p. 86)

Paragraph 3: b
Paragraph 4: c
Paragraph 6: a
Paragraph 7: *(Answers vary.)*
Paragraph 8: *(Answers vary.)*

Exercise C and D (p. 86) *(Answers vary.)*

5. WORK WITH THE VOCABULARY

Exercise A (p. 87)

1. c   2. e   3. f   4. a   5. b   6. d

Exercise B (p. 87)

1. unacceptable; acceptable
2. clean; unclean
3. available; unavailable
4. unfair; fair
5. unsafe; safe
6. Untruthful; truthful
7. broken; unbroken
8. unsatisfactory; satisfactory

Exercise C (p. 87)

monopolize – control

muckrakers – authors…wrote about wrongdoings by various companies

6. GET READY TO READ ABOUT: Consumer Protection Laws (p. 88)

(Answers vary.)

Use Your Reading Skills (p. 88)

1. advice column   3. *(Answers vary.)*
2. consumer rights   4. *(Answers vary.)*

8. PROCESS WHAT YOU READ (p. 90)

1. T   2. T   3. F   4. F   5. T

9. WORK WITH THE VOCABULARY (p. 90)

1. d   2. e   3. c   4. b   5. f   6. a
(Answers vary.)

10. GET READY TO READ AND SHARE

Exercise A and B (p. 91) *(Answers vary.)*

Exercise C (p. 91)
1. Text A: Advertising
   Text B: The Ad Council
2. *(Answers vary.)*

Exercise D (p. 91)
Text A:
1. Why We Buy
2. one of the most important influences on buying habits is advertising
3. *(Answers vary.)*

Text B:
1. Advertising for Ideas
2. the Ad Council sells ideas to the American public
3. *(Answers vary.)*

Exercise E (p. 91)
(See answers for Exercise A, p. 95)

13. SHARE WHAT YOU LEARNED

Focus Questions for Text A (p. 95)
1. print, television, and in the movies
2. causes them to spend more money
3. feelings of isolation and emptiness make "the good life" as shown in advertising seem very desirable
4. because it works

Focus Questions for Text B (p. 95)
1. it creates PSAs; to inform the public and help people change their behavior
2. forest fires caused by campers have decreased dramatically, and the number of acres lost to fire has gone from 22 million to 4 million per year
3. it increased seat belt usage from 21% to 73% and saved 85,000 lives
4. with the help of marketing executives and advertising agencies who contribute their time

14. SHARE WHAT YOU THINK (p. 95)
(Answers vary.)

15. REFLECT ON WHAT YOU READ IN THIS UNIT (p. 96) *(Answers vary.)*

Unit 7   Extreme Sports

WHAT DO YOU KNOW ABOUT EXTREME SPORTS? (p. 97) *(Answers vary.)*

1. GET READY TO READ ABOUT: Extreme Sports

Exercise A (p. 98)
1. snowboarding, skateboarding, surfing, and football
2. volleyball and baseball
3. *(Answers vary.)*

Exercise B (p. 86)
1. g   2. a   3. d   4. h
5. b   6. e   7. c   8. f

2. BUILDING READING SKILLS: Skimming

Practice Skimming
Exercise B (p. 99)
1. extreme skateboarding   2. no   3. b
Use Your Reading Skills
Exercise B (p. 100)
1. extreme sports   3. yes; more popular
2. yes   4. *(Answers vary.)*

4. PROCESS WHAT YOU READ

Exercise A (p. 102)
1. because risk and change have played an important role in American history
2. 1) Americans chose to fight the Revolutionary War against England in order to change the government, 2) pioneers moved west facing many difficulties and risks as they began their new lives; *(Answers vary.)*
3. a person who looks for risks and thrills; because it is made up of immigrants who are often risk takers and who look for excitement and adventure
4. nations that have a high number of immigrants
5. because they have a strong desire to live life fully and to experience all they can and risking their lives and surviving dangerous challenges makes them feel braver, stronger, and more self-confident

Exercise B (p. 102) *(Answers vary.)*

5. WORK WITH THE VOCABULARY

Exercise A (p. 102)
1. strong   2. goals   3. popular
4. declining   5. extreme

Exercise B (p. 102)
1. climber; climb; Climbing
2. skateboard; skateboarder; Skateboarding
3. Skydiving; skydive; skydiver
4. ski; skiing; skier

6. IMPROVING READING SPEED: Changing Reading Speed (p. 103)
(Answers vary.)

7. GET READY TO READ ABOUT: BASE Jumping (p. 103) *(Answers vary.)*

Use Your Reading Skills
Exercise A (p. 104)
1. an interview   3. *(Answers vary.)*
2. BASE Jumping   4. yes

Exercise B (p. 104) *(Answers vary.)*

9. PROCESS WHAT YOU READ

Exercise A (p. 106)
1. T   2. F   3. T   4. F   5. T
Exercise B (p.106)
2,6,1,3,5,4

10. WORK WITH THE VOCABULARY
(p. 106)
1. e   2. h   3. f   4. c
5. b   6. a   7. g   8. d

11. GET READY TO READ AND SHARE

Exercise A and B (p. 107) *(Answers vary.)*

Exercise C (p. 107)
1. biographical articles
2. Text A: Kristen Ulmer
   Text B: Mark Wellman

Exercise D (p. 107)
Text A:
1. Kristen Ulmer, who takes risks for a living
2. yes
3. no
4. *(Answers vary.)*

Text B:
1. Mark Wellman, who is a paraplegic and does extreme sports
2. no
3. yes
4. *(Answers vary.)*

Exercise E (p. 107)
(See answers for Exercise D above)

14. SHARE WHAT YOU LEARNED

Focus Questions for Text A (p. 97)
1. because she likes extreme sports and takes lots of risks
2. she has thrown her body off 70–foot cliffs, she skis 50–degree slopes, she is an ice-climber, paraglider and downhill mountain biker, and she is the only woman to have skied down Wyoming's Grand Teton; she got injuries to her knees and had knee surgery 5 times in 4 years
3. She survived a series of 100–200 mph avalanches. She was skiing with three other people on a 55–degree slope in France when the avalanche hit. She survived by clinging to the side of the mountain.
4. to "go big"; people shouldn't do things halfway

Focus Questions for Text B (p. 111)
1. because he is in a wheelchair
2. in a 100-foot fall while climbing a high peak; he lost the use of his legs and became a paraplegic
3. to climb El Capitan; he designed special clothing and equipment and trained himself—he swam, lifted weights, and practiced climbing
4. together they prepared and worked hard to climb El Capitan

14. SHARE WHAT YOU THINK
(p. 111) *(Answers vary.)*

15. REFLECT ON WHAT YOU READ IN THIS UNIT (p. 112)
(Answers vary.)

Unit 8   Staying in Touch

WHAT DO YOU KNOW ABOUT TELECOMMUNICATIONS? (p. 113)
(Answers vary.)

1. GET READY TO READ ABOUT:
   Telecommunications
Exercise A (p. 114)
1. T   2. F   3. T   4. F
5. T   6. F   7. F   8. F

Exercise B (p. 114)
1. a   2. b   3. b   4. a   5. c   6. c

2. BUILDING READING SKILLS:
   Identifying Patterns of Organization
Practice Identifying Patterns of Organization
Exercise A (p. 115)
1. sequence; before, after, before
2. list; in addition, also,

Exercise B (p. 115)
Paragraph 1: Before Bell completed his work…, only after Bell designed a transmitter…, Bell arrived two hours before Gray did…

Paragraph 2: In addition, they make it easy for new and old…, telecommunications also enables employees…

Use Your Reading Skills
Exercise A (p. 116)
1. Telecommunications in the U.S.
2. *(Answers vary.)*
3. *(Answers vary.)*

Exercise B (p. 116)
sequence; before, after that, Then after, Then, Soon after, Finally, First of all, Second, In addition, soon, Soon after, next, first, Then, Later, At first

4. PROCESS WHAT YOU READ
Exercise A (p. 118)
1. six months
2. 1944
3. Samuel Morse
4. 1876
5. Alexander Graham Bell
6. Global communications got its start in 1957.
7. a telecommunications system that linked computers, it allowed researchers at one university to access information from computers at another university and was the start of the Internet
8. 53%

Exercise B (p. 118) *(Answers vary.)*

5. WORK WITH THE VOCABULARY
   (p. 118)
decode – read
telegraph line – wires
replaced – took the place of
transmit – send
global – across the globe
linking – connecting
access – see and use
instantaneous – fast and easy

6. GET READY TO READ ABOUT:
   Cell Phones (p. 119) *(Answers vary.)*
Use Your Reading Skills
Exercise A (p. 119)
1. the New York Times; James Gorman
2. using cell phones in the wilderness
3. *(Answers vary.)*
4. *(Answers vary.)*

Exercise B (p. 119)
sequence

Exercise C (p. 119) *(Answers vary.)*

8. PROCESS WHAT YOU READ
Exercise A (p. 121)
1. T   2. T   3. T   4. F   5. F

Exercise B (p. 121)
3

Exercise C (p. 121) *(Answers vary.)*

9. WORK WITH THE VOCABULARY
Exercise A (p. 122)
1. d   2. e   3. g   4. a   5. f
6. i   7. c   8. h   9. b   10. j

Exercise B (p. 122)
1. d; *(Answers vary.)*
2. a; *(Answers vary.)*
3. b; *(Answers vary.)*
4. c; *(Answers vary.)*

Exercise C (p. 122)
a. hurt
b. woods
c. "Hi, honey, guess where I am?"

10. GET READY TO READ AND SHARE
Exercise A and B (p. 123) *(Answers vary.)*
Exercise C (p. 123)
1. Text A: the history of the telephone
   Text B: e-mail
2. *(Answers vary.)*

Exercise D (p. 123)
1. Text A: On March 10, 1876, Bell spoke the first words over the telephone.
   Text B: In 1971, e-mail was born.
2. *(Answers vary.)*

Exercise E (p. 123)
Text A: 1. date   2. sequence
        3. sequence   4. list

Text B: 1. date   2. sequence
        3. list   4. list

13. SHARE WHAT YOU LEARNED
Focus Questions for Text A (p. 127)
1. March 10, 1876 by Alexander Graham Bell
2. Bell spilled some acid on his clothing and called for help. His assistant, Watson, heard his voice over the telephone.
3. First people had phones in their homes. Then the pay phone was invented so people could make calls away from home. Then a cable under the Atlantic allowed North Americans to talk to people in Europe. Then came mobile phones and cell phones so people can stay in touch wherever they are. Now cell phones can even monitor a person's pulse and breathing rate.
4. phone calls often interrupt family time, unwanted calls come from telemarketers, many people expect employees or co-workers to be available any time by cell phone, people use cell phones while driving, which is dangerous

Focus Questions for Text B (p. 125)
1. 1971 by Ray Tomlinson
2. Tomlinson sent the first ten letters on the computer keyboard from his computer to his co-worker's computer.
3. messages can be transmitted in seconds, messages can be informal, short and to the point which takes less time, e-mail allows direct communication with heads of companies and government officials, people stay connected through e-mail, shy people can communicate their feelings more easily on e-mail
4. advertisers send unwanted messages, sometimes people accidentally send private messages to a long list of people, e-mail messages stay on the computer hard drive even after they are deleted

14. SHARE WHAT YOU THINK
   (p. 127) *(Answers vary.)*

15. REFLECT ON WHAT YOU READ IN THIS UNIT (p. 128)
(Answers vary)

Teacher's Notes

The Thinking Behind *Read and Reflect*

Read and Reflect follows current second-language reading pedagogy by ensuring that students:

- activate their background knowledge before and while they read,
- learn and apply effective reading strategies,
- read silently and with a purpose,
- interact with the material while they read,
- develop strategies to improve reading speed,
- expand their active and passive vocabulary,
- check their comprehension of a text,
- analyze, synthesize, and/or evaluate the author's ideas.

The texts in *Read and Reflect* are adapted from or modeled after authentic texts, such as newspaper and magazine articles, web pages, and encyclopedia articles. This is done to give intermediate-level students as real a reading experience as possible. The flow and voice of the original materials were retained in the adapted texts, while the vocabulary and grammar were adjusted to match the students' level.

In *Read and Reflect*, students are encouraged to read silently because the reading of a text is intended to be a silent interaction between the reader and the text (except in the case of poetry or reading to an audience). Although reading an individual word or single sentence aloud can help students' comprehension, reading an entire text aloud does not increase students' reading proficiency and is not emphasized in this book.

Read and Reflect also gives students the opportunity to practice improving their reading speed. Many students read so slowly (stopping to look up every word they don't know) that

by the time they come to the end of the paragraph, they have forgotten what they read at the beginning. Reading faster helps students better comprehend what they read. In fact, research shows that students need to read at about 200 words per minute in order to read effectively.

The variety of vocabulary exercises in *Read and Reflect* as well as the wealth of contextualized vocabulary in the texts, assist students in the development of active and passive vocabulary. Getting meaning from context is a key reading strategy. Right from the beginning, students are encouraged to determine the meaning of new words from context rather than relying on their dictionaries. While students are given the opportunity to work with a dictionary in some pre-reading activities, reliance on the dictionary *while* reading often prevents the experience from being fluent and effective. In addition, academic words (e.g., create, identify, respond, summarize, etc.) are introduced in order to help students prepare for academic reading in their English and content-based classes.

Book 2 of *Read and Reflect* lays a foundation for the development of critical literacy by having students examine the source of a text in relationship to the ideas and opinions expressed within the text. It also provides opportunities for students to consider and clarify their own opinions, attitudes, and values in relation to the text.

Teaching from *Read and Reflect*

Read and Reflect provides instructional flexibility, allowing you to tailor the activities to your classroom setting and your students' needs. One need universal to all students is to understand the purpose of their learning. The "To the Student" page (p. vi) introduces the purpose of this series and provides suggestions to help students read better. You can

also reinforce this concept in class, emphasize the goals of each unit before you teach it, and point out how students have met those goals at the end of the unit.

A Tour of the Unit

The unit tour below outlines the purpose of each type of activity and provides teaching suggestions.

OPENING PAGE

The goals on the opening page identify the unit's cultural theme and reading strategies. The cartoon or illustration on the page prompts students to think about and discuss what they already know about the theme of the unit.

Teaching Suggestions

- Give students time to think or write about their responses to discussion questions before they speak.
- Teach or review the appropriate language and non-verbal behavior associated with stating opinions and agreeing or disagreeing with others, before having students engage in the discussion activities on this page. One activity which ensures participation is to have one student respond to a question and have five or six other students create a chain of responses based on what the first student said. For example, if Jose says, "I think everyone who succeeds in school will succeed at work. What do you think, Pat?" Pat can say, "I agree with you. What do you think, Tanya?" Tanya may say, "I disagree. I think you can succeed at work without school. What do you think, Mario?" etc.

GET READY TO READ

Before reading the first and second texts of the unit, students complete pre-reading activities that activate their prior knowledge about the reading topics and expose them to key vocabulary.

Teaching Suggestions

- One type of vocabulary activity in this section has students work in pairs or teams to discuss the meanings of words they know from a list of key vocabulary. Then they look up the words they don't know in a dictionary. Encourage students to ask other teams or pairs to define words they don't know before looking them up.

BUILDING READING SKILLS

This page introduces important reading skills such as skimming or identifying patterns of organization, and explains the strategies students can use to implement these skills. For example, moving your eyes quickly down a page of text and not reading every word are strategies for skimming. This page also reviews and helps students refine more basic reading skills such as previewing and scanning. Improving Reading Speed and Comprehension exercises introduce strategies such as skipping words students don't know. After students practice the strategies, they apply the new reading strategies (as well as strategies from previous units) in the Use Your Reading Skills exercises. All reading skills and strategies are recycled within units and throughout the book in order to give students the maximum opportunity to learn and use the skills.

Teaching Suggestions

- Provide an example of the reading skill and strategies in the unit before students read about them. For example, for previewing, show students a newspaper headline or picture and have them tell you what the newspaper article is about. Name the strategy students are employing and explain the rationale for using it. Elicit situations in which students have used the same strategy.

- Periodically review the strategies the students have learned. Ask students to monitor their use of these strategies in their reading outside of class and encourage students to identify the ways these strategies help their reading comprehension.

READ

The four theme-related texts in each unit help students deepen their understanding of the theme, read with greater comprehension, and internalize recycled vocabulary. The first text is typically a more academic text such as an encyclopedia or textbook article. The second text is usually lighter in tone and often has a more conversational style, such as an interview or personal essay. Beginning in Unit 3, students time their reading of Text 2 in order to practice reading faster. The third and fourth texts are part of the Read and Share activity (see next page) but may also be taught as independent texts.

Important vocabulary in the texts is introduced in the pre-reading activities or presented in context. Difficult content words that are key to students' understanding of a text but are not high frequency words, are glossed. Words that are not important to a general understanding of a text are left undefined and students are expected to skip over them.

Teaching Suggestions

- To help students get the most meaning from their reading, show them how to use the glossaries on the page, and then ask them to read the text once silently. Tell them to read without looking up unknown words.

- Set a time limit for students to read the text and answer the questions. A time limit requires students to finish at the same time so that they can begin their pair or group work simultaneously.

- Give students the rationale for timing their reading of Text 2 (Unit 3 and after) (see page 136, The Thinking Behind *Read and Reflect*, paragraph 4 for rationale). Have students note their start time and end time in the spaces provided. Once they finish reading students should go directly to section A of the Process What You Read questions. It is important that students answer the questions on their own and check their answers in the answer key. Then students

should look at the inside back cover for instructions on finding their reading speed and recording both their reading speed and their comprehension score. Students should look at the comprehension score and reading speed together. It is important to improve reading speed while at the same time keeping comprehension high. Keeping track of both will help students understand the importance of reading speed and encourage them to improve it.

- Once the processing questions have been answered and checked, you can read the text aloud to the class while they follow along silently. As you read, model some "think aloud" techniques, such as asking yourself the following types of questions aloud, *I wonder if that's true?* or *What is the author telling me?* This will help students understand the thinking processes used by effective readers.

PROCESS WHAT YOU READ

After reading the first and second text in each unit, students do exercises to check their comprehension and use their higher-level thinking skills to analyze or evaluate the information they read. The first time an exercise type is introduced in the book, a sample answer is given.

Teaching Suggestions

- For the first exercise of this section, encourage students to do the exercise individually first, and then to look back at the text to check their answers with a partner or teammates. Explain that this procedure will help them evaluate how much of the text they understood. As a final check, students can look at the answer key. (See the READ section above for guidance on using comprehension questions with timed readings.)

- For sentence-level writing practice, have students write out answers to questions in their notebooks.

- In this section there is usually a second exercise, which is intended to help students think critically about the text. To ensure that every student has a chance to think about the topic, tell students to first answer the questions individually, and then discuss their answers with a partner, a small group, or the whole class.

- In order to help develop students' critical literacy, each article has brief introductory material identifying its source or background. To help students develop critical literacy, ask them questions such as: *Why does the author include the opinions of people both for and against the use of Native American names and symbols?* (Unit 2, Text 3) or *Do encyclopedia articles usually have facts or opinions?* (Unit 6, Text 1).

WORK WITH THE VOCABULARY

After reading the first and second text in each unit, students increase their active vocabulary through a variety of exercises. These include working with definitions, synonyms, word families, prefixes, suffixes, and context clues.

Teaching Suggestions

- Encourage students to keep a journal of vocabulary words including those presented in this section, the glossed words, and other words from the text. Then have students note each time they encounter these words in their reading outside of class.

- Key vocabulary words are often recycled in subsequent units but it is helpful if you recycle the words in other activities you do with your class. This will increase the likelihood of new words becoming part of your students' active vocabulary.

READ AND SHARE

These four pages comprise a highly effective and communicative technique for developing reading proficiency. The Read and Share technique follows these steps:

Get Ready to Read and Share

1. Students complete general pre-reading and vocabulary activities.

2. They preview two complimentary texts in order to select one to read.

3. Along with the information gleaned in their preview, the students use guiding questions and open-ended statements to learn more about the text they selected.

Read A/Read B

4. Students choose a topic to read and read the text with the purpose of learning new information and then sharing it with a partner.

Share What You Learned

5. When the class finishes reading, each student finds a partner who has read the same text and they work in pairs to answer the focus questions relating to their text.

6. Students then work with a partner that has read the complimentary text. The pairs take turns sharing what they have read, using the focus questions to guide their presentation.

Share What You Think

7. In small groups or as a whole class, students use what they have learned from the texts as well as their background knowledge and personal experience to respond to follow-up questions.

Teaching Suggestions

- Each time students do a Read and Share activity, remind them of the purpose for the activity. Tell students that during the Read and Share they will choose one of two texts and work with a partner to answer questions about the text. Once they understand the most important ideas in their text, they will share these ideas with a pair of students who read the other text.

- This activity works best if students choose their own text; however, this can be tricky if most students prefer one text over another (20 students pick A, 3 pick B). If fewer than a third of the students pick one of the texts, ask for volunteers to read the less popular text, assuring students

that they can read their first choice the next time. If you prefer not to leave the selection to chance, you can assign A/B roles to students.

- To give students an additional reading opportunity, you can assign the complimentary text as an in-class activity or as homework.

- From time to time you may want to have all students read the A and B texts sequentially instead of as a Read and Share activity. In this case, have students read one text and answer the corresponding focus questions. It may be helpful to put the focus questions for the selected text on the board or overhead. Then repeat the process for the other text.

REFLECT ON WHAT YOUR READ IN THIS UNIT

This page provides three types of activities that help students synthesize the ideas within the unit: interviewing, charting, and writing. In the interview activity, students work in pairs or small groups to ask and answer questions that relate their personal experiences to the cultural focus of the unit. For the charting activity, students create charts and diagrams that show their responses to questions about an aspect of the unit's cultural focus. The writing activity uses these charts or questions to guide students in writing paragraphs that reflect the unit theme.

In alternating units, students are also prompted to research a topic they've read about or to reflect on their use of the reading strategies they have learned. In the research activity students use the Internet or an encyclopedia to read more about a unit topic, take notes, and report back to the class on the information they find. The reading strategy reflection chart helps students identify which strategies they use and which they need to practice more. Students who actually use the strategies they learn greatly improve their skill in reading.